CONTENTS

ICE CREAM CONE RATTLES

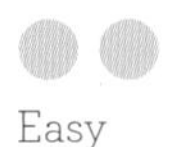
Easy

MEASUREMENTS

Approx 7"/18cm tall

MATERIALS

Yarn

Bernat® *Softee® Baby™ Solids,* 5oz/140g balls, each approx 362yd/331m (acrylic)

- 1 ball in #30010 Little Mouse (A)
- 1 ball in #02004 Mint or #30205 Prettiest Pink or:

Bernat® *Softee® Baby™ Ombres,* 4.2oz/120g balls, each 310yd/283m (acrylic)

- 1 ball in #31320 Lavender Lullaby Ombre (B)

Hook

- Size E/4 (3.5mm) crochet hook, *or size needed to obtain gauge*

Notions

- Small plastic fillable egg
- Small amount of dried rice or beans
- 1 pair of 6mm plastic safety eyes
- Small amount of black embroidery floss for mouth
- Embroidery needle

GAUGE

18 sc and 19 rows = 4"/10cm using size E/4 (3.5mm) crochet hook. *TAKE TIME TO CHECK GAUGE.*

CONE

With A, ch 2.

1st rnd: 4 sc in 2nd ch from hook. Join with sl st to first sc.

2nd rnd: Ch 1. 1 sc in each sc around. Join with sl st to first sc.

3rd rnd: Ch 1. 2 sc in each each sc around. Join with sl st to first sc. 8 sc.

4th and 5th rnds: Ch 1. 1 sc in each sc around. Join with sl st to first sc.

6th rnd: Ch 1. 2 sc in first sc. 1 sc in next sc. *2 sc in next sc. 1 sc in next sc. Rep from * around. Join with sl st to first sc. 12 sc.

7th and 8th rnds: As 4th and 5th rnds.

9th rnd: Ch 1. 2 sc in first sc. 1 sc in next sc. *2 sc in next sc. 1 sc in next sc. Rep from * around. Join with sl st to first sc. 18 sc.

10th and 11th rnds: As 4th and 5th rnds.

12th rnd: Ch 1. 2 sc in first sc. 1 sc in each of next 2 sc. *2 sc in next sc. 1 sc in each of next 2 sc. Rep from * around. Join with sl st to first sc. 24 sc.

13th and 14th rnds: As 4th and 5th rnds.

15th rnd: Ch 1. 2 sc in first sc. 1 sc in each of next 3 sc. *2 sc in next sc. 1 sc in each of next 3 sc. Rep from * around. Join with sl st to first sc. 30 sc.

16th and 17th rnds: As 4th and 5th rnds.

18th rnd: Ch 1. 2 sc in first sc. 1 sc in each of next 4 sc. *2 sc in next sc. 1 sc in each of next 4 sc. Rep from * around. Join with sl st to first sc. 36 sc.

19th to 26th rnds: Ch 1. 1 sc in each sc around. Join with sl st to first sc. Fasten off at end of last rnd.

Stuff Cone.

SCOOP

With B, ch 2.

1st rnd: 8 sc in 2nd ch from hook. Join with sl st to first sc.

2nd rnd: Ch 1. 2 sc in each sc around. Join with sl st to first sc. 16 sc.

3rd rnd: Ch 1. 1 sc in each sc around. Join with sl st to first sc.

ICE CREAM CONE RATTLES

4th rnd: Ch 1. 2 sc in first sc. 1 sc in next sc. *2 sc in next sc. 1 sc in next sc. Rep from * around. Join with sl st to first sc. 24 sc.

5th rnd: As 3rd rnd.

6th rnd: Ch 1. 2 sc in first sc. 1 sc in each of next 2 sc. *2 sc in next sc. 1 sc in each of next 2 sc. Rep from * around. Join with sl st to first sc. 32 sc.

7th rnd: As 3rd rnd.

8th rnd: Ch 1. 2 sc in first sc. 1 sc in each of next 3 sc. *2 sc in next sc. 1 sc in each of next 3 sc. Rep from * around. Join with sl st to first sc. 40 sc.

9th to 16th rnds: Ch 1. 1 sc in each sc around. Join with sl st to first sc.

17th rnd: Ch 1. *1 sc in each of next 8 sc. Sc2tog. Rep from * around. Join with sl st to first sc. 36 sc.

18th rnd: Ch 1. 1 sc in each st around. Join with sl st to first sc. Do not fasten off.

FINISHING

Attach safety eyes as shown in picture. With black embroidery floss, embroider mouth. Fill plastic egg approx halfway with dried rice or beans. Secure egg opening with tape. Stuff Scoop, inserting egg and stuff around egg.

Join Scoop to Cone

1st rnd: With bottom edge of Scoop and top edge of Cone aligned, ch 1. Working through both thicknesses, work 1 rnd of sc in each ec around, inserting more stuffing as you go. Join with sl st to first sc.

2nd rnd: Skip first sc. *5 dc in next sc. Skip next sc. Sl st in next sc. Skip next sc. Rep from * around. Join with sl st to first dc. Fasten off. •

DREAMY CLOUDS BLANKET

Easy

MEASUREMENTS

Approx 43"/109cm × 45"/114.5cm

MATERIALS

Yarn 

Bernat® *Pipsqueak*™, 3½oz/100g balls, each approx 101yd/92m (polyester)

- 5 balls in #59128 Baby Blue (A)
- 3 balls in #59005 Whitey White (B)

Hook

- Size J/10 (6mm) crochet hook, or size needed to obtain gauge

GAUGE

8 dc and 6 rows = 4"/10cm using size J/10 (6mm) hook.

TAKE TIME TO CHECK GAUGE.

NOTES

- Blanket is worked diagonally from corner to corner.
- When working from chart, wind small balls of the colors to be used, one for each separate area of color in the design. Start new colors at appropriate points.
- To change color, work to last 2 loops on hook, yoh with new color. Pull through 2 loops on hook to complete st and proceed in new color.

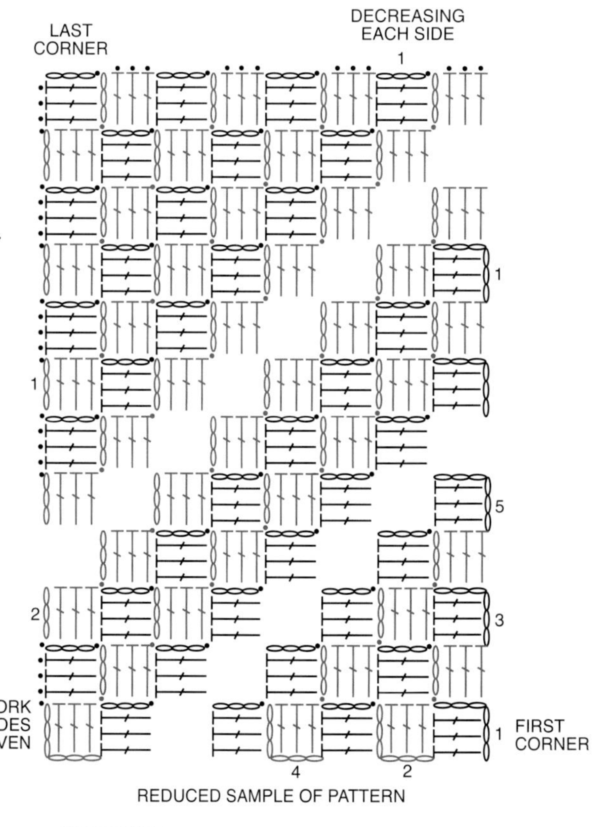

DREAMY CLOUDS BLANKET

BLANKET

With A, ch 6.

1st row: (RS). 1 dc in 4th ch from hook (counts as 2 dc). 1 dc in each of last 2 ch. Turn. 1 block made.

2nd row: Ch 6. 1 dc in 4th ch from hook. 1 dc in each of next 2 ch—beg block made. (Sl st. Ch 3. 3 dc) in next ch-3 sp—block made. Turn. 2 blocks.

3rd row: Beg block. *Block in next ch-3 sp. Rep from * to end of row. Turn. 3 blocks.

Keeping cont of color changes in Chart (each square on grid represents 1 block), rep last row until 33rd row of Chart is complete. 33 blocks. See Chart below.

Keeping cont of Chart, proceed as follows to work sides even:

34th row: Beg block. *Block in next ch-3 sp. Rep from * to last ch-3 sp. Sl st in last ch-3 sp. (Do not make a block.) Turn.

Keeping cont of Chart, proceed as follows to dec corner:

35th row: Sl st in each of rst 3 dc. *Block in next ch-3 sp. Rep from * to last ch-3 sp. Sl st in last ch-3 sp. (Do not make a block.) Turn.

Keeping cont of Chart, rep last row until 1 block rem. Fasten off.

FINISHING

Edging

With RS facing, join B with sl st between any 2 blocks along edge.

1st rnd: Ch 3. *Sl st between next 2 blocks. Ch 3. Rep from * around, working (Sl st. Ch 3. Sl st) in each corner. Join with sl st in same sp as rst sl st.

2nd rnd: Sl st in rst ch-3 sp. Ch 3 (counts as dc). 2 dc in same ch-3 sp. *3 dc in next ch-3 sp. Rep from * to around, working (3 dc. Ch 1. 3 dc) in each corner ch-3 sp. Join with sl st to top of beg ch-3.

Fasten off. •

CHART

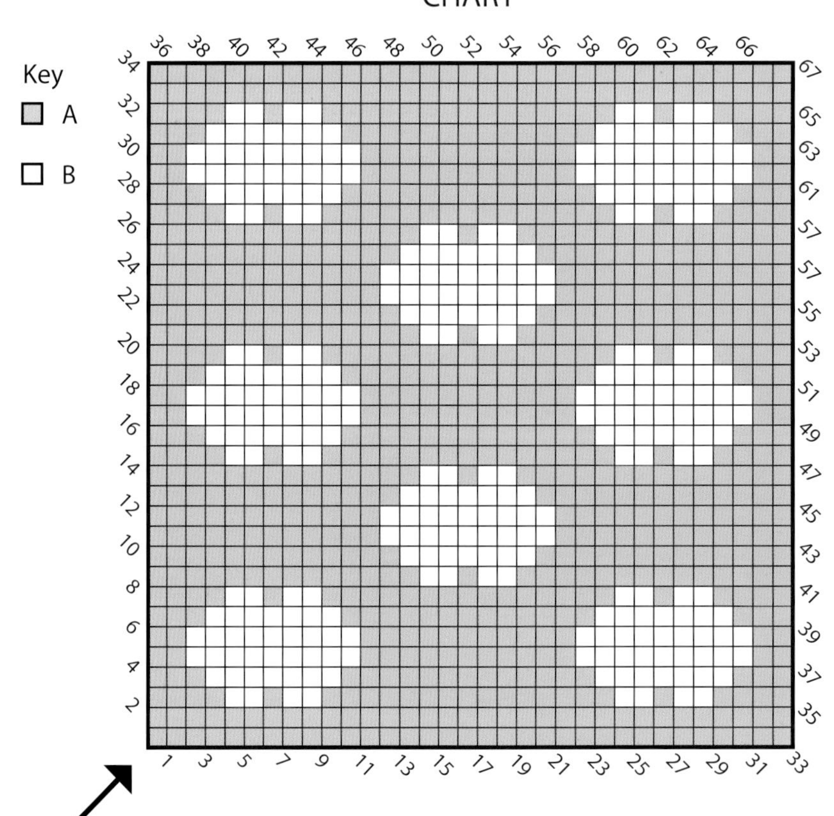

CLOUDY DAY MOBILE

Easy

MEASUREMENTS

Approx 12"/30.5cm × 33"/84cm

MATERIALS

Yarn 

Bernat® *Baby Blanket*™, 3½oz/100g balls, each approx 72yd/65m (polyester)

- 3 balls in #03008 Vanilla (A)
- 1 ball in #03734 Baby Teal (B)
- 1 ball in #03736 Seafoam (C)

Hook

- Size L/11 (8mm) crochet hook, *or size needed to obtain gauge*

Notions

- 12"/30cm embroidery hoop
- 1"/2.5cm split ring
- Stuffing

GAUGE

7 sc and 8 rows = 4"/10cm using size L/11 (8mm) hook.
TAKE TIME TO CHECK GAUGE.

NOTES

- Ch 3 at beg of rnd counts as dc.
- See diagrams on page 10.

MOBILE

Small Cloud (make 4 pieces alike)

With A, ch 4. Join with sl st to first ch to form ring.

1st rnd: Ch 3. 11 dc in ring. Join with sl st to top of ch 3. 12 dc.

2nd rnd: (Sl st in next dc. 4 dc in next dc) 6 times. Sl st in first dc. Fasten off.

Medium Cloud (make 4 pieces alike)

With A, ch 4. Join with sl st to first ch to form ring.

1st rnd: Ch 3. 11 dc in ring. Join with sl st to top of ch 3. 12 dc.

2nd rnd: Ch 3. 1 dc in same sp as last sl st. 2 dc in each dc around. Join with sl st to top of ch 3. 24 dc.

3rd rnd: (Sl st in next dc. Skip 1 dc. 5 dc in next dc. Skip 1 dc) 6 times. Sl st in first dc. Fasten off.

Large Cloud (make 4 pieces alike)

With A, ch 4. Join with sl st to first ch to form ring.

1st rnd: Ch 3. 11 dc in ring. Join with sl st to top of ch 3. 12 dc.

2nd rnd: Ch 3. 1 dc in same sp as last sl st. 2 dc in each dc around. Join with sl st to top of ch 3. 24 dc.

3rd rnd: Ch 3. 1 dc in same sp as last sl st. 2 dc in each dc around. Join with sl st to top of ch 3. 48 dc.

4th rnd: (Sl st in next dc. Skip 2 dc. 5 dc in next dc. Skip 2 dc) 8 times. Sl st in first dc. Fasten off.

Joining Back and Front of Clouds

Place WS of 2 pieces tog. Join yarn with sl st to same sp as last sl st. Working through both thicknesses, ch 1. 1 sc in same sp as sl st. 1 sc in each sp around, stuffing lightly as you work. Join with sl st to first sc. Fasten off.

Hanging Loops

With A, make 6 chains, alternating lengths from 3"/7.5cm to 6"/15cm. Attach to top of Clouds as shown in photo.

Raindrops (make 6 each with B and C)

Ch 4. Join with sl st to first ch to form ring.

1st rnd: Ch 1. (8 sc. Ch 1. 2 dc. Ch 1. 2 sc) all in ring. Join with sl st to first sc. Fasten off, leaving a

CLOUDY DAY MOBILE

12"/30.5cm tail. Using tail, attach Raindrops to Clouds as pictured (3 on Large Clouds, 2 on Medium Clouds, and one on Small Clouds), alternating lengths from 3"/7.5cm to 8"/20.5cm.

FINISHING

Using hanging loops, mount Clouds around embroidery hoop evenly. Make 3 crochet chains 24"/61cm long, and attach them around hoop evenly spaced. Join chains in center of hoop with split ring, as pictured. •

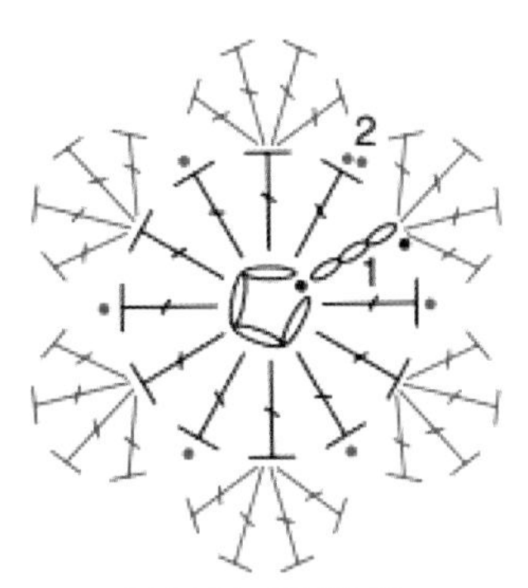

SMALL CLOUD

STITCH KEY

- = chain (ch)
- • = slip stitch (sl st)
- = single crochet (sc)
- = double crochet (dc)

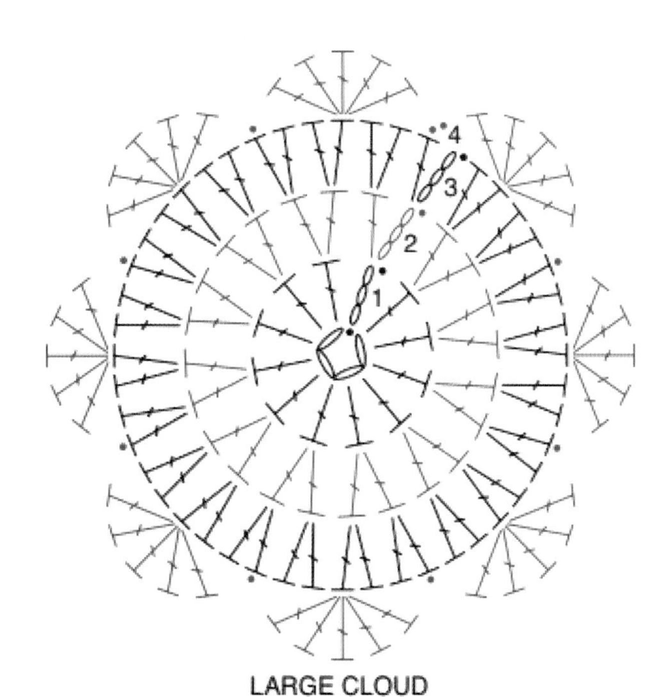

LARGE CLOUD

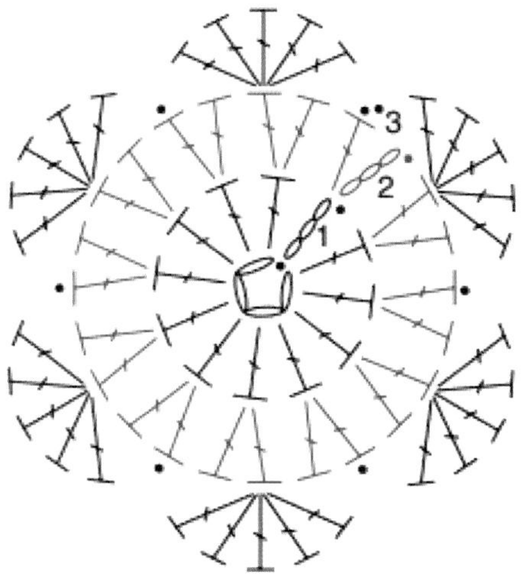

MEDIUM CLOUD

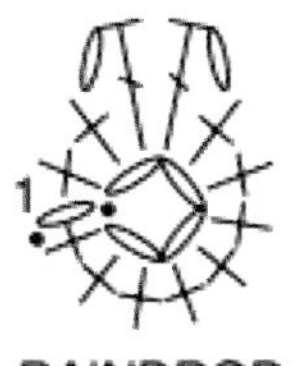

RAINDROP

BUNNY FLOOR PILLOW

Easy

MEASUREMENTS
42"/106.5cm long x 16"/40.5cm high

MATERIALS
Yarn  

Bernat® *Baby Blanket*™, 10½oz/300g balls, each approx 220yd/201m (polyester)

- 10 balls in #04008 Vanilla (A)

Yarn

Bernat® *Baby Blanket*™, 3½oz/100g balls, each approx 72yd/65m (polyester)

- 2 balls in #03010 Baby Sand (B)
- 2 balls in #03200 Baby Pink (C)

Hook

- Size Q (16mm) crochet hook, *or size needed to obtain gauge*

Notions

- Stitch markers
- Tapestry needle
- 5lbs/2.3kg stuffing

GAUGE
6 sc and 5 rnds = 4"/10cm using size Q (16mm) hook with 3 strands of yarn held together.

TAKE TIME TO CHECK GAUGE.

FRONT LEG (MAKE 2)
With 3 strands of B, ch 2.

1st rnd: 8 sc in 2nd ch from hook. Join with sl st to first sc. 8 sts.

2nd rnd: Ch 1. 2 sc in each sc around. Join with sl st to first sc. 16 sts.

3rd rnd: Ch 1. 1 sc in same sp as last sl st. *2 sc in next sc. 1 sc in next sc. Rep from * to last sc. 2 sc in last sc. Join 3 strands of A with sl st to first sc. 24 sts.

BUNNY FLOOR PILLOW

4th rnd: With A, ch 1. *Working in back loops only,* 1 sc in each sc around. Join with sl st to first sc.

5th to 13th rnds: Ch 1. 1 sc in each sc around. Join with sl st to first sc

Fasten off.

Make second Front Leg. Set aside.

BACK LEG (MAKE 2)

With 3 strands of B, ch 2.

1st rnd: 8 sc in 2nd ch from hook. Join with sl st to first sc. 8 sts.

2nd rnd: Ch 1. 2 sc in each scaround. Join with sl st to first sc. 16 sts.

3rd rnd: Ch 1. 1 sc in same sp as last sl st. *2 sc in next sc. 1 sc in next sc. Rep from * to last sc. 2 sc in last sc. 24 sts.

4th rnd: Ch 1. 1 sc in same sp as last sl st. 2 sc in next sc. *1 sc in each of next 2 sc. 2 sc in next sc. Rep from * around to last sc. 1 sc in last sc. Join 3 strands of A with sl st to first sc. 32 sts.

5th rnd: With A, ch 1. Working in back loops only, 1 sc in each sc around. Join with sl st to first sc.

6th to 15th rnds: Ch 1. 1 sc in each sc around. Join with sl st to first sc.

Fasten off.

Make second Back Leg, but do not fasten off.

Note: *Do not* join rnds.

Place marker to indicate beg of rnd, moving marker up each rnd throughout Body stuffing Back Legs and Body as you work.

Join Body

With 3 strands of A, work 12 sc across second Back Leg. Work 28 sc across first Back Leg. Skip next 4 sts of Second Back Leg for instep. Work 1 sc in each of rem 16 sc of Second Back Leg. 56 sc. Leave 4 rem sts of First Back Leg unworked for instep. 4 sts rem unworked on each leg at center Body.

BODY

Work 24 rnds even in sc.

Shape Body

1st rnd: *1 sc in each of next 6 sc. Sc2tog. Rep from * around. 49 sts.

2nd rnd: *1 sc in each of next 5 sts. Sc2tog. Rep from * around. 42 sts.

3rd rnd: *1 sc in each of next 4 sts. Sc2tog. Rep from * around. 35 sts.

4th rnd: *1 sc in each of next 3 sts. Sc2tog. Rep from * around. 28 sts.

5th rnd: *1 sc in each of next 2 sts. Sc2tog. Rep from * around. 21 sts. Stuff Body firmly.

6th rnd: *1 sc in next st. Sc2tog. Rep from * around. 14 sts.

7th rnd: *Sc2tog. Rep from * around.

Fasten off.

INNER EAR (MAKE 2)

With 3 strands of C, ch 12.

1st row: (WS). 1 sc in 2nd ch from hook. 1 sc in each of next 9 ch. 3 sc in last ch. Working into opposite side of foundation ch, 1 sc in each of next 10 ch. Turn.

2nd row: (RS). Ch 1. 1 sc in each of next 4 sc. 1 hdc in each of next 6 sc. 2 hdc in each of next 3 sc. 1 hdc in each of next 6 sc. 1 sc in each of last 4 sc.

Fasten off.

OUTER EAR (MAKE 2)

With 3 strands of A, ch 12.

Work 1st and 2nd rows as given for Inner Ear.

3rd row: Ch 1. 1 sc in each st to end of row. Turn.

Join Ears

4th row: Position Inner and Outer Ear with WS tog and Inner Ear in front. Ch 1. Working through both thicknesses, 1 sc in each st to end of row.

Fasten off, leaving a tail to sew Ear to Head.

HEAD

With 3 strands of A, ch 2.

Note: Do not join rnds. Place marker to indicate beg of

rnd, moving marker up each rnd throughout Head.

1st rnd: 6 sc in 2nd ch from hook.

2nd rnd: 2 sc in each sc around. 12 sts.

3rd rnd: *1 sc in next st. 2 sc in next st. Rep from * around. 18 sts.

4th rnd: *1 sc in each of next 5 sts. 2 sc in next st. Rep from * around. 21 sts.

5th rnd: *1 sc in each of next 6 sts. 2 sc in next st. Rep from * around. 24 sts.

6th rnd: *1 sc in each of next 3 sts. 2 sc in next st. Rep from * around. 30 sts.

7th rnd: *1 sc in each of next 4 sts. 2 sc in next st. Rep from * around. 36 sts.

8th rnd: 1 sc in each sc around.

9th rnd: *1 sc in each of next 5 sts. 2 sc in next st. Rep from * around. 42 sts.

10th rnd: *1 sc in each of next 6 sts. 2 sc in next st. Rep from * around. 48 sts.

11th to 17th rnds: 1 sc in each sc around.

18th rnd: *1 sc in each of next 6 sts. Sc2tog. Rep from * around. 42 sts.

19th rnd: *1 sc in each of next 5 sts. Sc2tog. Rep from * around. 36 sts.

20th rnd: *1 sc in each of next 4 sts. Sc2tog. Rep from * around. 30 sts.

21st rnd: *1 sc in each of next 3 sts. Sc2tog. Rep from * around. 24 sts.

Stuff Head firmly.

22nd rnd: *1 sc in each of next 2 sts. Sc2tog. Rep from * around. 18 sts.

23rd rnd: *1 sc in next st. Sc2tog. Rep from * around. 12 sts.

Complete stuffing Head.

24th rnd: *Sc2tog. Rep from * around. 6 sts.

Fasten off.

FINISHING

Make 7"/18cm pompom with A for Tail and sew to Body. Sew Ears to Head. With B and C, embroider face details with satin stitch and straight stitch. Stuff Front Legs and sew to top of Body. Sew Head above Front Legs. Sew 4 instep sts of back legs tog. •

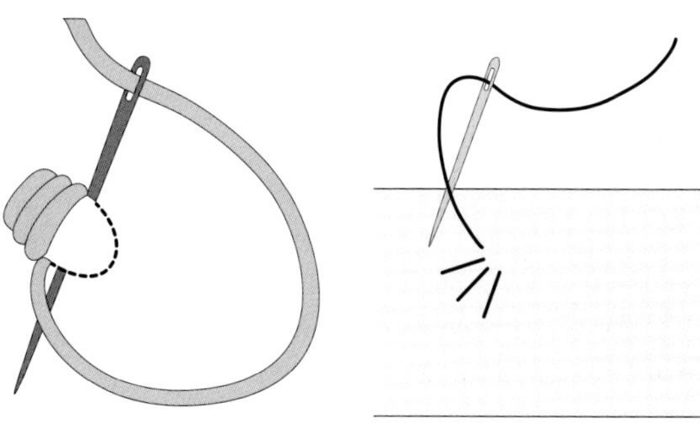

ELEPHANT BASKET

Easy

MEASUREMENTS

Approx 9"/23cm diameter × 7"/18cm tall, excluding trunk

MATERIALS

Yarn 

Bernat® *Baby Blanket*™, 3½oz/100g balls, each approx 72yd/65m (polyester)

- 3 balls in #03200 Baby Pink

Hook

- Size J/10 (6mm) crochet hook, *or size needed to obtain gauge*

Notions

- Stitch marker
- Stuffing
- Small amount of smooth black yarn for embroidery

GAUGE

10 sc and 11 rows = 4"/10cm using size J/10 (6mm) hook. *TAKE TIME TO CHECK GAUGE.*

BASKET

Note: Join each rnd with sl st to first sc.

Ch 2.

1st rnd: 8 sc in 2nd ch from hook. Join. 8 sc.

2nd rnd: Ch 1. 2 sc in each sc around. Join. 16 sts.

3rd rnd: Ch 1. *2 sc in next sc. 1 sc in next sc. Rep from * around. Join. 24 sts.

4th rnd: Ch 1. *2 sc in nextsc. 1 sc in each of next 2 sc. Join. 32 sts.

5th rnd: Ch 1. *2 sc in nextsc. 1 sc in each of next 3 sc. Join. 40 sts.

6th rnd: Ch 1. *2 sc in nextsc. 1 sc in each of next 4 sc. Join. 48 sts.

7th rnd: Ch 1. *2 sc in nextsc. 1 sc in each of next 5 sc. Join. 56 sts.

8th rnd: Ch 1. *2 sc in nextsc. 1 sc in each of next 6 sc. Join. 64 sts.

9th rnd: Ch 1. *Working in back loops only,* 1 sc in each sc around. Join. Place marker at end of rnd.

10th rnd: Ch 1. *1 sc in each sc around. Join.

Rep last rnd until work from marked row measures 7"/18cm.

Next rnd: Ch 1. *Working from right to left instead of left to right as usual,* 1 reverse sc in each sc around. Join. Fasten off.

TRUNK

Note: Trunk is worked in spiral. *Do not* join rnds. Place marker on first st to mark beg of each rnd.

Ch 20. Join with sl st to first ch to form ring.

1st rnd: Ch 1. 1 sc in each ch around. 20 sc.

2nd and 3rd rnds: 1 sc in each sc around.

4th rnd: *Sc2tog. 1 sc in each of next 3 sc. Rep from * around. 16 sc.

5th to 7th rnds: 1 sc in each sc around.

8th rnd: *Sc2tog. 1 sc in each of next 2 sc. 12 sc.

9th to 11th rnds: 1 sc in each sc around.

12th rnd: *Sc2tog. 1 sc in next sc. Rep from * around. 8 sc.

13th rnd: 1 sc in each sc around.

Rep last rnd until work from beg measures 22"/56cm. Fasten off.

EARS

Ch 2.

1st row: 4 sc in 2nd ch from hook. Turn.

2nd row: Ch 1. 2 sc in each sc to end of row. 8 sc. Turn.

3rd row: Ch 1. *2 sc in next sc. 1 sc in next sc. Rep from * to end of row. 12 sc. Turn.

4th row: Ch 1. *2 sc in next sc. 1 sc in each of next 2 sc. Rep from * to end of row. 16 sc. Do not turn.

5th row: Ch 1. *Working from right to left instead of left to right as usual,* 1 reverse sc in each sc around. Join with sl st to first sc.

FINISHING

Lightly stuff Trunk. Sew Trunk and Ears to Basket as shown in photo. With smooth black yarn, embroider eyes with satin stitch as shown in photo. •

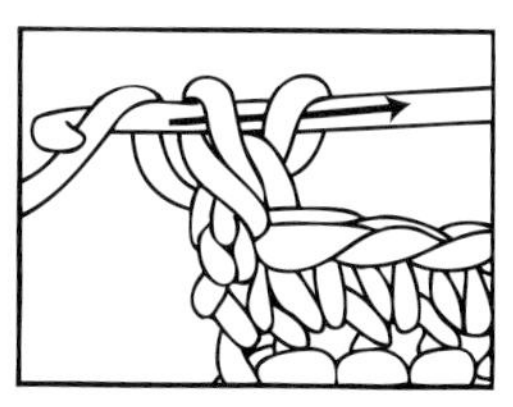

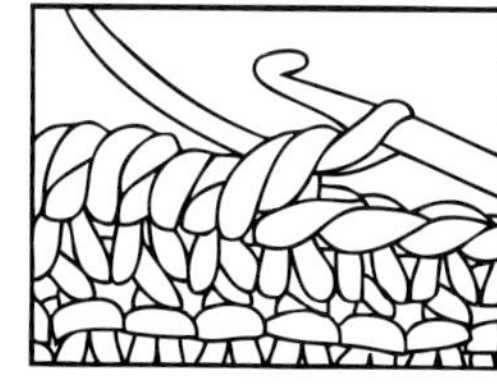

REVERSE SINGLE CROCHET

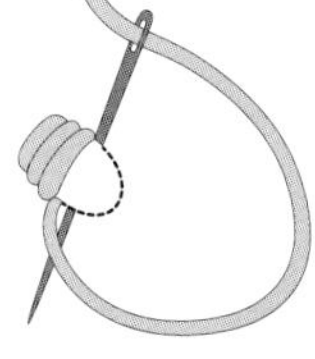

SATIN STITCH

UNICORN STUFFIE

Easy

MEASUREMENTS

Approx 10"/25.5cm tall × 9"/23cm diameter, excluding limbs and horn

MATERIALS

Yarn 

Bernat® *Baby Velvet™*, 10½oz/300g balls, each approx 492yd/450m (polyester)

- 1 ball in #86018 Cuddly Cloud (A)
- 1 ball in #86030 Bleached Aqua (B)
- 1 ball in #86001 Joyful Gold (C)
- 1 ball in #86029 Potpourri (D)

Hook

- Size D/3 (3.25mm) crochet hook, *or size needed to obtain gauge*

Notions

- Stuffing
- Yarn needle
- Split-lock stitch count markers
- 2 × 14mm safety eyes
- Small amount of black worsted-weight yarn for embroidery

GAUGE

18 sc and 20 rows = 4"/10cm using size D/3 (3.25mm) hook.

TAKE TIME TO CHECK GAUGE.

NOTES

- Stuffie is worked in a continuous spiral. *Do not* join at end of rnds. Place marker on first st of rnd and move marker each rnd to keep place.
- To change colors, work to last 2 loops on hook and draw new color through last 2 loops and proceed.

BODY

With A, ch 2.

1st rnd: 8 sc in 2nd ch from hook, placing marker on first st for beg of rnd. Do not join. 8 sc.

2nd rnd: 2 sc in each sc around. 16 sc.

3rd rnd: *2 sc in next sc. 1 sc in next sc. Rep from * around. 24 sc.

4th rnd: *2 sc in next sc. 1 sc in each of next 2 sc. Rep from * around. 32 sc.

5th rnd: *2 sc in next sc. 1 sc in each of next 3 sc. Rep from * around. 40 sc.

6th rnd: *1 sc in each of next 2 sc. 2 sc in next sc. 1 sc in each of next 2 sc. Rep from * around. 48 sc.

7th rnd: *2 sc in next sc. 1 sc in each of next 5 sc. Rep from * around. 56 sc.

8th rnd: *1 sc in each of next 3 sc. 2 sc in next sc. 1 sc in each of next 3 sc. Rep from * around. 64 sc.

9th rnd: *2 sc in next sc. 1 sc in each of next 7 sc. Rep from * around. 72 sc.

10th rnd: 1 sc in each sc around.

11th rnd: *1 sc in each of next 4 sc. 2 sc in next sc. 1 sc in each of next 4 sc. Rep from * around. 80 sc.

12th rnd: *2 sc in first sc. 1 sc in each of next 9 sc. Rep from * around. 88 sc.

13th rnd: 1 sc in each sc around.

14th rnd: *1 sc in each of next 5 sc. 2 sc in next sc. 1 sc in each of next 5 sc. Rep from * around. 96 sc.

15th rnd: *2 sc in first sc. 1 sc in each of next 11 sc. Rep from * around. 104 sc.

16th rnd: 1 sc in each sc around.

17th rnd: *1 sc in each of next 6 sc. 2 sc in next sc. 1 sc in each of next 6 sc. Rep from * around. 112 sc.

18th rnd: *2 sc in first sc. 1 sc in each of next 13 sc. Rep from * around. 120 sc.

19th rnd: 1 sc in each sc around. Place 2nd marker at end of rnd—*do not* move 2nd marker each rnd.

UNICORN STUFFIE

Rep last rnd until work from 2nd marker measures 4"/10cm.

Shape Top as Follows

1st rnd: *Sc2tog. 1 sc in each of next 13 sc. Rep from * around. 112 sc.

2nd to 4th rnds: 1 sc in each sc around.

5th rnd: *Sc2tog. 1 sc in each of next 12 sc. Rep from * around. 104 sc.

6th to 8th rnds: 1 sc in each sc around.

9th rnd: *Sc2tog. 1 sc in each of next 11 sc. Rep from * around. 96 sc.

10th and 11th rnds: 1 sc in each sc around.

12th rnd: *Sc2tog. 1 sc in each of next 10 sc. Rep from * around. 88 sc.

13th rnd: 1 sc in each sc around.

14th rnd: *Sc2tog. 1 sc in each of next 9 sc. Rep from * around. 80 sc.

15th rnd: 1 sc in each sc around.

16th rnd: *1 sc in each of next 4 sc. Sc2tog. 1 sc in each of next 4 sc. Rep from * around. 72 sc.

17th rnd: 1 sc in each sc around.

18th rnd: *Sc2tog. 1 sc in each of next 7 sc. Rep from * around. 64 sc.

19th rnd: 1 sc in each sc around.

20th rnd: *1 sc in each of next 3 sc. Sc2tog. 1 sc in each of next 3 sc. Rep from * around. 56 sc.

21st rnd: 1 sc in each sc around.

22nd rnd: *Sc2tog. 1 sc in each of next 5 sc. Rep from * around. 48 sc.

23rd rnd: 1 sc in each sc around.

24th rnd: *1 sc in each of next 2 sc. Sc2tog. 1 sc in each of next 2 sc. Rep from * around. 40 sc.

Insert Safety Eyes. Stuff Body and Head.

25th rnd: 1 sc in each sc around.

26th rnd: *Sc2tog. 1 sc in each of next 3 sc. Rep from * around. 32 sc.

21st rnd: *1 sc in next sc. Sc2tog. 1 sc in next sc. Rep from * around. 24 sc.

22nd rnd: *Sc2tog. 1 sc in next sc. Rep from * around. 16 sc.

23rd rnd: *Sc2tog. Rep from * around. 8 sc.

Fasten off leaving a long end. Thread end through rem sts and fasten securely.

EARS (MAKE 2 EACH WITH A AND B)

Ch 10.

1st row: (RS). 1 sc in 2nd ch from hook. 1 sc in each ch to end of chain. 9 sc. Turn.

2nd and alt rows: Ch 1. 1 sc in each sc to end of row. Turn.

3rd row: Ch 1. Sc2tog. 1 sc in each of next 5 sc. Sc2tog. 7 sc. Turn.

4th row: Ch 1. Sc2tog. 1 sc in each of next 3 sc. Sc2tog. 5 sc. Turn.

5th row: Ch 1. Sc2tog. 1 sc in next sc. Sc2tog. 3 sc. Turn.

6th row: Ch 1. Sc3tog. Fasten off.

Join Ears

Hold one A Ear and one B Ear tog with WS facing each other. Hold B side facing to work joining row. Join A with sl st through both thicknesses to bottom right corner of Ears.

1st row: (RS). Ch 1. Working through both thicknesses, work 8 sc evenly up right side of Ear to corner. 3 sc in corner. Work 8 sc evenly down left side of Ear. Fasten off.

SNOUT

With A, ch 5. Working in spiral as given for Body, proceed as follows:

1st rnd: 1 sc in 2nd ch from hook. 1 sc in each of next 2 ch. 3 sc in last ch. *Working across opposite side of foundation ch,* 1 sc in each of next 2 ch. 2 sc in last ch. 10 sc.

2nd rnd: 2 sc in first sc. 1 sc in each of next 2 sc. 2 sc in each of next 3 sc. 1 sc in each of next 2 sc. 2 sc in each of last 2 sc. 16 sc.

3rd rnd: 1 sc in first sc. 2 sc in next sc. 1 sc in each of next 3 sc. (2 sc in next sc. 1 sc in next sc) 3 times. 1 sc in each of next 2 sc. 2 sc in next sc. 1 sc in next sc. 2 sc in next sc. 22 sc.

4th rnd: *Working in back loops only,* 1 sc in each sc around.

5th to 7th rnds: *Working in both loops,* 1 sc in each sc around.

Fasten off. Stuff Snout lightly.

HOOVES (MAKE 4)

With B, ch 2. Working in spiral as for Body, proceed as follows:

1st rnd: 8 sc in 2nd ch from hook. Place marker on last st for beg of rnd. 8 sc.

2nd rnd: 2 sc in each sc around. 16 sc.

3rd rnds: *2 sc in next sc. 1 sc in next sc. Rep from * around. 24 sc.

4th rnd: *2 sc in next sc. 1 sc in each of next 2 sc. Rep from * around. 32 sc.

5th rnd: *Working in back loops only,* 1 sc in each sc around.

6th and 7th rnds: *Working in both loops,* 1 sc in each sc around.

8th rnd: *Sc2tog. 1 sc in each of next 2 sc. Rep from * around. 24 sc.

9th rnd: 1 sc in each sc around.

10th rnd: *Sc2tog. 1 sc in next sc. Rep from * around. Break B. 16 sc. Join A with sl st to back loop only of any sc.

11th rnd: With A, and working in back loops only, 1 sc in each sc around.

12th to 15th rnds: Working in both loops, 1 sc in each sc around.

Fasten off. Stuff Hoof lightly.

Create Cloven Hoof

Thread yarn needle with length of B. Draw yarn through center of hoof base (middle of 1st rnd) and up to top of 10th rnd (at color change). Cinch tightly to form cloven hoof. Secure ends. Repeat for each Hoof.

HORN

With A, ch 2. Working in spiral as for Body, proceed as follows:

1st rnd: 4 sc in 2nd ch from hook. 4 sc.

2nd rnd: 2 sc in each sc around. Rep from * around. 8 sc.

3rd rnd: 1 sc in each sc around.

4th rnd: *2 sc in next sc. 1 sc in each of next 2 sc. Rep from * around. 12 sc.

5th and 6th rnds: 1 sc in each sc around.

7th rnd: *2 sc in first sc. 1 sc in each of next 3 sc. Rep from * around. 16 sc.

8th and 9th rnds: 1 sc in each sc around.

10th rnd: *1 sc in each of next 4 sc. 2 sc in next sc. Rep from * around. 20 sc.

11th to 18th rnds: 1 sc in each sc around. Fasten off. Stuff Horn lightly.

MANE

**With D, ch 32.

1st row: With D, 2 dc in 4th ch from hook. 3 dc in each ch to end of chain, joining C to last st. 1 Curl made. Break D.

2nd row: With C, ch 32. 2 dc in 4th ch from hook. 3 dc in each ch to end of chain, joining B to last st. Break C.

3rd row: With B, ch 32. 2 dc in 4th ch from hook. 3 dc in each ch to end of chain, joining D to last st. Break C.**

Rep last 3 rows 3 times more. 12 Curls made. Fasten off.

TAIL

Work from ** to ** as given for Mane. 3 Curls made. Fasten off.

FINISHING

Sew Ears, Snout, Hooves, and Horn to Body as seen in photo. With A, create nostrils by making 2 tight stitches in Snout, and tacking them to Body. Fold Mane in half, having 6 Curls on each side. Beg at center point behind Horn, sew Mane to Body in straight line down the back. Group ends of 3 Curls of Tail tog and sew to back of Body as seen in photo. With black worsted weight yarn, embroider eyebrows and mouth using Stem Stitch. •

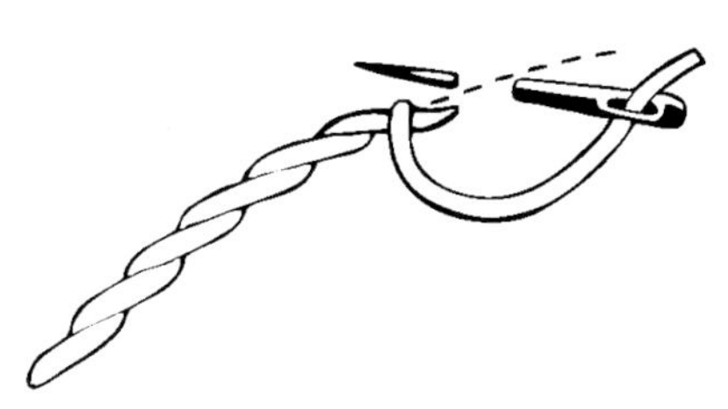

STEM STITCH

TWINKLE STAR PILLOW

Easy

MEASUREMENTS
Approx 18"/45.5cm from point to point

MATERIALS
Yarn 

Bernat® *Baby Velvet™*, 10½oz/300g balls, each approx 492yd/450m (polyester)
- 1 ball in #86018 Cuddly Cloud or #86016 Misty Gray

Hook
- Size G/6 (4mm) crochet hook, *or size needed to obtain gauge*

Notion
- Stuffing

GAUGE
14 dc and 8 rows = 4" [10 cm].
TAKE TIME TO CHECK GAUGE.

STITCH GLOSSARY
Dcfp Yoh and draw up a loop around post of next stitch at front of work, inserting hook from right to left. (Yoh and draw through 2 loops on hook) twice.

FRONT AND BACK (MAKE ALIKE)
Note: Ch 3 at beg of rnd/row counts as dc.
Ch 4.
1st rnd: 9 dc in 4th ch from hook (skipped ch-3 counts as dc). Join with sl st to top of ch-3. 10 dc.
2nd rnd: Ch 3. 1 dc in first dc (counts as 2 dc). 3 dc in next dc. *2 dc in next dc. 3 dc in next dc. Rep from * around. Join with sl st to top of ch-3. 25 dc.
3rd rnd: Ch 3. 1 dc in first dc. 1 dc in next dc. 2 dc in next dc. 1 dc in next dc. 1 dcfp around next dc. *(2 dc in next dc. 1 dc in next dc) twice. 1 dcfp around next dc. Rep from * around. Join with sl st to top of ch-3. 35 sts.
4th rnd: Ch 3. 1 dc in first dc. 1 dc in each of next 2 dc. 2 dc in next dc. 1 dc in each of next 2 dc. 1 dcfp around next dcfp. *(2 dc in next dc. 1 dc in each of next 2 dc) twice. 1 dcfp around next dcfp. Rep from * around. Join with sl st to top of ch-3. 45 dc.
5th rnd: Ch 3. 1 dc in first dc. 1 dc in each of next 3 dc. 2 dc in next dc. 1 dc in each of next 3 dc. 1 dcfp around next dcfp. *(2 dc in next dc. 1 dc in each of next 3 dc) twice. 1 dcfp around next dcfp. Rep from * around. Join with sl st to top of ch-3. 55 dc.
6th rnd: Ch 3. 1 dc in first dc. 1 dc in each of next 4 dc. 2 dc in next dc. 1 dc in each of next 4 dc. 1 dcfp around next dcfp. *(2 dc in next dc. 1 dc in each of next 4 dc) twice. 1 dcfp around next dcfp. Rep from * around. Join with sl st to top of ch-3. 65 dc.
7th rnd: Ch 3. 1 dc in first dc. 1 dc in each of next 5 dc. 2 dc in next dc. 1 dc in each of next 5 dc. 1 dcfp around next dcfp. *(2 dc in next dc. 1 dc in each of next 5 dc) twice. 1 dcfp around next dcfp. Rep from * around. Join with sl st to top of ch-3. 75 dc.

8th rnd: Ch 3. 1 dc in first dc. 1 dc in each of next 6 dc. 2 dc in next dc. 1 dc in each of next 6 dc. 1 dcfp around next dcfp. *(2 dc in next dc. 1 dc in each of next 6 dc) twice. 1 dcfp around next dcp. Rep from * around. Join with sl st to top of ch-3. 85 dc.

9th rnd: Ch 3. 1 dc in first dc. 1 dc in each of next 7 dc. 2 dc in next dc. 1 dc in each of next 7 dc. 1 dcfp around next dcfp. *(2 dc in next dc. 1 dc in each of next 7 dc) twice. 1 dcfp around next dcfp. Rep from * around. Join with sl st to top of ch-3. 95 dc.

10th rnd: Ch 3. 1 dc in first dc. 1 dc in each of next 8 dc. 2 dc in next dc. 1 dc in each of next 8 dc. 1 dcfp around next dcfp. *(2 dc in next dc. 1 dc in each of next 8 dc. 2 dc in next dc) twice. 1 dcfp around next dcfp. Rep from * around. Join with sl st to top of ch-3. 105 dc. Do not fasten off.

Make 1st Point

1st row: (RS). Ch 3. 1 dc in each of next 20 sts. Turn. 21 dc.

2nd row: Ch 3. 1 dc in next dc (counts as Dc2tog). 1 dc in each dc to last 2 dc. Dc2tog. Turn. 19 dc.

Rep last row 8 times more. 3 dc rem.

Next row: (RS). Ch 3. Dc2tog. Fasten off.

Make 2nd to 5th Points

With RS facing, join yarn with sl st to next rem unworked dc of rnd 10. Work as given for 1st Point.

FINISHING

With WS of Front and Back facing each other, join yarn with sl st to last st of any Point.

1st rnd: Ch 1. Working through both thicknesses, work 1 sc evenly around edge of Pillow working 3 dc in last st of each point and sc2tog at base of each Point (where Points meet), stuffing as you go. Join with sl st to first sc. •

PURRRFECT PLAY RUG

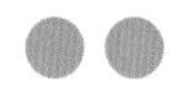
Easy

MEASUREMENTS

Approx 35"/89cm in diameter

MATERIALS

Yarn (6)

Bernat® *Baby Blanket™*, 10½oz/300g balls, each approx 220yds/201m (polyester)

• 4 balls in #04010 Baby Sand (A)

Yarn (6)

Bernat® *Baby Blanket™*, 3½oz/100g balls, each approx 72yds/65m (polyester)

• 1 ball in #03008 Vanilla (B)

• 1 ball in #03200 Baby Pink (C)

Hooks

• Size N/15 (10mm) and L/11 (8mm) crochet hooks, *or size needed to obtain gauge*

GAUGE

6 dc and 4 rows = 4"/10 cm with yarn held double and using larger hook. *TAKE TIME TO CHECK GAUGE.*

NOTE

Ch 3 at beg of rnd counts as dc.

RUG

Face

With 2 strands of A held tog and larger hook, ch 4. Join with sl st to first ch to form ring.

1st rnd: Ch 3. 11 dc in ring. Join with wl st to top of ch 3. 12 dc.

2nd rnd: Ch 3. 1 dc in first dc. 2 dc in each dc around. Join with sl st to top of ch 3. 24 dc.

3rd rnd: Ch 3. 1 dc in first dc. 1 dc in next dc. *2 dc in next dc. 1 dc in next dc. Rep from * around. Join with sl st to top of ch 3. 36 dc.

4th rnd: Ch 3. 1 dc in first dc. 1 dc in each of next 2 dc. *2 dc in next dc. 1 dc in each of next 2 dc. Rep from * around. Join with sl st to top of ch 3. 48 dc.

5th rnd: Ch 3. 1 dc in first dc. 1 dc in each of next 3 dc. *2 dc in next dc. 1 dc in each of next 3 dc. Rep from * around. Join with sl st to top of ch 3. 60 dc.

6th rnd: Ch 3. 1 dc in first dc. 1 dc in each of next 4 dc. *2 dc in next dc. 1 dc in each of next 4 dc. Rep from * around. Join with sl st to top of ch 3. 72 dc.

7th rnd: Ch 3. 1 dc in first dc. 1 dc in each of next 5 dc. *2 dc in next dc. 1 dc in each of next 5 dc. Rep from * around. Join with sl st to top of ch 3. 84 dc.

8th rnd: Ch 3. 1 dc in first dc. 1 dc in each of next 6 dc. *2 dc in next dc. 1 dc in each of next 6 dc. Rep from * around. Join with sl st to top of ch 3. 96 dc.

9th rnd: Ch 3. 1 dc in first dc. 1 dc in each of next 7 dc. *2 dc in next dc. 1 dc in each of next 7 dc. Rep from * around. Join with sl st to top of ch 3. 108 dc.

Cont as established, inc 12 dc every rnd until piece measures approx 35"/89cm in diameter. Fasten off.

Ears (make 2)

With 2 strands of A held tog and larger hook, ch 18.

1st row: 1 sc in 2nd ch from hook. 1 sc in each ch to end of chain. Turn. 17 sc.

2nd row: Ch 1. 1 sc in each sc to end of row. Turn.

3rd row: Ch 1. Sc2tog. 1 sc in each sc to last 2 sc. Sc2tog. Turn. 15 sts.

4th row: Ch 1. 1 sc in each st to end of row. Turn.

Rep last 2 rows to 3 sts.

Next row: Ch 1. Sc3tog. Fasten off.

PURRRFECT PLAY RUG

Inner Ear (make 2)

With 1 strand of C and smaller hook, ch 14.

1st row: 1 sc in 2nd ch from hook. 1 sc in each ch to end of chain. Turn. 13 sc.

2nd row: Ch 1. Sc2tog. 1 sc in each sc to last 2 sc. Sc2tog. 11 sts.

3rd row: Ch 1. 1 sc in each st to end of row. Turn.

Rep last 2 rows to 3 sts.

Next row: Ch 1. Sc3tog. Fasten off.

Sew Inner Ear to Ear as shown in picture.

Eyes (make 2)

With 1 strand of B and smaller hook, ch 4.

****1st rnd:** 9 dc in 4th ch from hook. Join with sl st to top of ch 3. 10 dc.

2nd rnd: Ch 3 (counts as dc). 1 dc in first dc (counts as 2 dc). 2 dc in each dc around. Join with sl st to top of ch 3. 20 dc.**

3rd rnd: Ch 3 (counts as dc). 1 dc in first dc (counts as 2 dc). 1 dc in next dc. *2 dc in next dc. 1 dc in next dc. Rep from * around. Join with sl st to top of ch 3. 30 dc. Fasten off.

Pupils (make 2)

With 1 strand of A and smaller hook, ch 4. Work from ** to ** as given for Eye. Fasten off. Sew Pupil to Eye as shown in picture.

Nose

With 1 strand of C and smaller hook, ch 9.

1st row (RS): 1 sc in 2nd ch from hook. 1 sc in each ch to end of chain. Turn. 8 sc.

2nd row: Ch 1. Sc2tog. 1 sc in each sc to last 2 sc. Sc2tog.

Turn. 6 sts.

3rd row: As 2nd row. 4 sts.

4th row: Ch 1. (Sc2tog) twice. 2 sts.

5th row: Ch 1. Sc2tog. Do not fasten off.

Ch 1. Work 1 rnd of sc around 3 edges, working 3 sc in each corner. Join with sl st to first sc. Fasten off.

FINISHING

Sew Eyes, Nose and Ears to Face as shown in picture.

Mouth

With 2 strands of B and smaller hook, ch 30. Fasten off.

With 2 strands of B and smaller hook, ch 15. Fasten off

Sew longer chain to Face, starting at tip of Nose and curving up to form Mouth. Sew shorter chain to form other side of Mouth.

Whiskers (make 4)

With 2 strands of B and smaller hook, ch 12. Fasten off.

Sew 2 Whiskers on either side of face as shown in picture. •

THREE SUSHI TOYS

Intermediate

MATERIALS

Yarn

Caron® *Simply Soft®*, 6 oz/170g balls, each approx 313yd/288m (acrylic)

- 1 ball in #9701 White (A)
- 1 ball in #9727 Black (B)
- 1 ball in #9754 Persimmon (C)
- 1 ball in #9765 Pumpkin (D)
- 1 ball in #9771 Chartreuse (E)

Hook

- Size G/6 (4mm) crochet hook, *or size needed to obtain gauge*

Notion

- Stuffing

GAUGE

17 hdc and 12 rows = 4"/10cm using size G/6 (4mm) hook.

TAKE TIME TO CHECK GAUGE.

NOTE

Ch 2 at beg of rnds does not count as a st.

MAKI ROLL

With A, ch 3.

1st rnd: 10 hdc in 3rd ch from hook. Join with sl st to first hdc. 10 hdc.

2nd rnd: Ch 2. 2 hdc in each hdc around. Join with sl st to first hdc. 20 hdc.

3rd rnd: Ch 2. 1 hdc in first hdc. *2 hdc in next hdc. 1 hdc in next hdc. Rep from * to last st. 2 hdc in last hdc. Join with sl st to first hdc. 30 hdc.

4th rnd: Ch 2. *1 hdc in each of next 2 hdc. 2 hdc in next hdc. Rep from * around. Join with sl st to first hdc. 40 hdc.

5th rnd: Ch 2. *1 hdc in each of next 3 hdc. 2 hdc in next hdc. Rep from * around. Join with sl st to first hdc. 50 hdc.

6th rnd: Ch 2. *1 hdc in each of next 4 hdc. 2 hdc in next hdc. Rep from * around. With B, join with sl st to first hdc. 60 hdc.

7th rnd: Ch 2. *Working in back loops only,* 1 hdc in each st around. Join with sl st to first hdc.

8th rnd: Ch 2. 1 hdc in each hdc around. Join with sl st to first hdc.

Rep 8th rnd until work from 7th rnd measures approx 4"/10cm. Join A at end of last rnd.

Shape Top

Next rnd: With A, ch 2. *Working in back loops only,* 1 hdc in each of first 4 hdc. *Hdc2tog. 1 hdc in each of next 4 hdc. Rep from * to last 2 sts. Hdc2tog. Join with sl st to first hdc. 50 sts.

Next rnd: Ch 2. 1 hdc in each of first 3 hdc. *Hdc2tog.

SHRIMP NIGIRI

MAKI ROLL

HAND ROLL

1 hdc in each of next 3 hdc. Rep from * to last 2 sts. Hdc2tog. Join with sl st to first hdc. 40 sts.
Next rnd: Ch 2. 1 hdc in each of first 2 hdc. *Hdc2tog. 1 hdc in each of next 2 hdc. Rep from * to last 2 sts. Hdc2tog. Join with sl st to first hdc. 30 sts.
Stuff Maki Roll.
Next rnd: Ch 2. 1 hdc in first hdc. *Hdc2tog. 1 hdc in next hdc. Rep from * to last 2 sts. Hdc2tog. Join with sl st to first hdc. 20 sts.
Next rnd: Ch 2. (Hdc2tog) 10 times. Join with sl st to first hdc. 10 sts.
Fasten off leaving a long end. Draw end tightly through rem sts and fasten securely.

Avocado (make 2)

With E, ch 8.
1st row: 1 sc in 2nd ch from hook. 1 sc in each ch to end of ch. Turn. 7 sc.
2nd row: Ch 1. Sc2tog. 1 sc in each of next 3 sc. Sc2tog. Turn. 5 sc.
3rd row: Ch 1. 1 sc in each sc to end of row. Turn.
4th row: Ch 1. Sc2tog. 1 sc in next sc. Sc2tog. Turn. 3 sc.
5th row: Ch 1. 1 sc in each sc to end of row.
Fasten off.

Salmon (make 2)

With C, ch 6.
1st row: 1 sc in 2nd ch from hook. 1 sc in each ch to end of ch. Turn. 5 sc.
2nd to 4th rows: Ch 1. 1 sc in each sc to end of row. Turn.
Fasten off.

Carrot (make 2)

With D, ch 3.
1st row: 5 hdc in 3rd ch from hook. Turn.
2nd row: Ch 2. 2 hdc in first hdc. 1 hdc in each hdc to end of row.
Fasten off.

FINISHING

Sew 1 each of Avocado, Salmon, and Carrot to top and bottom of Maki Roll. With A, embroider mouth and eyes as shown in picture.

SHRIMP NIGIRI

Rice

Note: Turn at end of each rnd to work RS and WS rnds.
With A, ch 6.
1st rnd: (RS). 3 hdc in 3rd ch from hook. 1 hdc in each of next 2 ch. 6 hdc in last ch. *Working into opposite side of foundation ch,* 1 hdc in each of next 2 ch. 3 hdc in last ch. Join with sl st to first hdc. Turn. 16 hdc.
2nd rnd: (WS). Ch 2. 1 hdc in first hdc. 3 hdc in next hdc. 1 hdc in each of next 4 hdc. 3 hdc in next hdc. 1 hdc in each of next 2 hdc. 3 hdc in next hdc. 1 hdc in each of next 4 hdc. 3 hdc in next hdc. 1 hdc in next hdc. Join with sl st to first hdc. Turn.
3rd rnd: Ch 2. 1 hdc in each of first 2 hdc. 3 hdc in next hdc. 1 hdc in each of next 6 hdc. 3 hdc in next hdc. 1 hdc in each of next 4 hdc. 3 hdc in next hdc. 1 hdc in each of next 6 hdc. 3 hdc in next hdc. 1 hdc in each of next 2 hdc. Join with sl st to first hdc. Turn.
4th rnd: Ch 2. 1 hdc in each of first 3 hdc. 3 hdc in next hdc. 1 hdc in each of next 8 hdc. 3 hdc in next hdc. 1 hdc in each of next 6 hdc. 3 hdc in next hdc. 1 hdc in each of next 8 hdc. 3 hdc in next hdc. 1 hdc in each of next 3 hdc. Join with sl st to first hdc. Turn.
5th rnd: Ch 2. 1 hdc in each of first 4 hdc. 3 hdc in next hdc. 1 hdc in each of next 10 hdc. 3 hdc in next hdc. 1 hdc in each of next 8 hdc. 3 hdc in next hdc. 1 hdc in each of next 10 hdc. 3 hdc in next hdc. 1 hdc in each of next 4 hdc. Join with sl st to first hdc. Turn.
6th rnd: Ch 2. *Working in front loops only,* 1 hdc in each hdc around. Join with sl st to first hdc. Turn.
7th rnd: Ch 2. 1 hdc in each hdc around. Join with sl st to first hdc. Turn.
Rep last rnd until work from 6th rnd measures approx 5 1/2"/14cm, ending on a RS rnd.
Next rnd: (WS). Ch 2. *Working in front loops only,* 1 hdc in each of first 4 hdc. Hdc3tog. 1 hdc in each of next 10 hdc. Hdc3tog. 1 hdc in each of next 8 hdc. Hdc3tog. 1 hdc in each of next 10 hdc. Hdc3tog. 1 hdc in each of next 4 hdc. Join with sl st to first hdc. Turn.

Next rnd: Ch 2. 1 hdc in each of first 3 hdc. Hdc3tog. 1 hdc in each of next 8 hdc. Hdc3tog. 1 hdc in each of next 6 hdc. Hdc3tog. 1 hdc in each of next 8 hdc. Hdc3tog. 1 hdc in each of next 3 hdc. Join with sl st to first hdc. Turn.

Next rnd: Ch 2. 1 hdc in each of first 2 hdc. Hdc3tog. 1 hdc in each of next 6 hdc. Hdc3tog. 1 hdc in each of next 4 hdc. Hdc3tog. 1 hdc in each of next 6 hdc. Hdc3tog. 1 hdc in each of next 2 hdc. Join with sl st to first hdc. Turn.

Next rnd: Ch 2. 1 hdc in first hdc. Hdc3tog. 1 hdc in each of next 4 hdc. Hdc3tog. 1 hdc in each of next 2 hdc. Hdc3tog. 1 hdc in each of next 4 hdc. Hdc3tog. 1 hdc in next hdc. Join with sl st to first hdc. Turn.

Next rnd: Ch 2. Hdc3tog. 1 hdc in each of next 2 hdc. (Hdc3tog) twice. 1 hdc in each of next 2 hdc. Hdc3tog. Join with sl st to first hdc.

Fasten off, leaving a long end. Draw end tightly through rem sts and fasten securely.

Shrimp

With C, ch 2.

1st rnd: 10 sc in 2nd ch from hook. Join with sl st to first sc. 10 sc.

2nd rnd: Ch 1. 2 sc in each sc around. Join with sl st to first sc. 20 sc.

3rd rnd: Ch 1. 1 sc in first sc. *2 sc in next sc. 1 sc in next sc. Rep from * to last st. 2 sc in last sc. Join with sl st to first sc. 30 sc.

4th rnd: Ch 1. 1 sc in each of first 2 sc. *2 sc in next sc. 1 sc in each of next 2 sc. Rep from * to last st. 2 sc in last sc. Join with sl st to first sc. 40 sc.

5th and 6th rnds: Ch 1. 1 sc in each sc around. Join with sl st to first sc.

7th rnd: Ch 1. 1 sc in each sc around. Join with sl st to first sc. Do not break C. Join A.

8th and 9th rnds: With A, ch 2. 1 hdc in first sc. 1 hdc in each of next 12 hdc. 1 sc in next sc. 1 sl st in each of next 2 sc. 1 sc in nextsc. 1 hdc in each of next 13 sc. Join with sl st to first hdc.

10th rnd: Ch 2. 1 hdc in first st. 1 hdc in each of next 12 sts. 1 sc in next st. 1 sl st in each of next 2 sts. 1 sc in next st. 1 hdc in each of next 13 sts. Join with sl st to first hdc. *Do not* break A, Join C.

11th and 12th rnds: With C, ch 1. 1 sc in each st around. Join with sl st to first sc.

THREE SUSHI TOYS

13th rnd: Ch 1. 1 sc in each st around. Join with sl st to first sc. *Do not* break C. Join A.

14th and 15th rnds: With A, ch 2. 1 hdc in each st around. Join with sl st to first hdc.

16th rnd: Ch 2. 1 hdc in each st around. Join with sl st to first hdc. *Do not* break A, Join C.

Rep 11th to 16th rnds once more. Break A.

Next 3 rnds: With C, ch 1. 1 sc in each st around. Join with sl st to first sc.

Next rnd: Ch 1. 1 sc in each of first 2 sc. *Sc2tog. 1 sc in each of next 2 sc. Rep from * to last 2 sts. Sc2tog. Join with sl st to first sc. 30 sts.

Next rnd: Ch 1. 1 sc in each st around. Join with sl st to first sc.

Next rnd: Ch 1. 1 sc in first sc. *Sc2tog. 1 sc in next sc. Rep from * to last 2 sts. Sc2tog. Join with sl st to first sc. 20 sts.

Next 2 rnds: Ch 1. 1 sc in each st around. Join with sl st to first sc.

Next rnd: Ch 1. (Sc2tog) 10 times. Join with sl st to first sc. 10 sts.

Next rnd: Ch 1. 1 sc in each st around. Join with sl st to first sc. Fasten off. With A, embroider line down center of Shrimp.

Tail (make 2).

With C, ch 10.

1st rnd: 1 hdc in 3rd ch from hook. 1 hdc in each of next 6 ch. 6 hdc in last ch. *Working into opposite side of foundation chain,* 1 hdc in each of next 7 ch. Fasten off.

FINISHING

Sew Tail to end of Shrimp.

With A, chain stitch through both thicknesses down center of Shrimp. Sew Shrimp to Rice as shown in picture. With B, embroider face on Shrimp Nigiri as shown in picture.

HAND ROLL

With B, ch 3.

1st rnd: 4 hdc in 3rd ch from hook. Join with sl st to first hdc. 4 hdc.

2nd rnd: Ch 2. 2 hdc in each hdc around. Join with sl st to first hdc. 8 hdc.

3rd rnd: Ch 2. 1 hdc in each hdc around. Join with sl st to first hdc.

4th rnd: Ch 2. 1 hdc in first hdc. *2 hdc in next hdc. 1 hdc in next hdc. Rep from * to last st. 2 hdc in last hdc. Join with sl st to first hdc. 12 hdc.

5th rnd: As 3rd rnd.

6th rnd: Ch 2. 1 hdc in each of first 2 hdc. *2 hdc in next hdc. 1 hdc in each of next 2 hdc. Rep from * to last st. 2 hdc in last hdc. Join with sl st to first hdc. 16 hdc.

7th rnd: As 3rd rnd.

8th rnd: Ch 2. 1 hdc in each of first 3 hdc. *2 hdc in next hdc. 1 hdc in each of next 3 hdc. Rep from * to last st. 2 hdc in last hdc. Join with sl st to first hdc. 20 hdc.

9th rnd: As 3rd rnd.

10th rnd: Ch 2. 1 hdc in each of first 4 hdc. *2 hdc in next hdc. 1 hdc in each of next 4 hdc. Rep from * to last st. 2 hdc in last hdc. Join with sl st to first hdc. 24 hdc.

11th rnd: As 3rd rnd.

12th rnd: Ch 2. 1 hdc in each of first 5 hdc. *2 hdc in next hdc. 1 hdc in each of next 5 hdc. Rep from * to last st. 2 hdc in last hdc. Join with sl st to first hdc. 28 hdc.

13th rnd: As 3rd rnd.

14th rnd: Ch 2. 1 hdc in each of first 6 hdc. *2 hdc in next hdc. 1 hdc in each of next 6 hdc. Rep from * to last st. 2 hdc in last hdc. Join with sl st to first hdc. 32 hdc.

15th rnd: As 3rd rnd.

16th rnd: Ch 2. 1 hdc in each of first 7 hdc. *2 hdc in next hdc. 1 hdc in each of next 7 hdc. Rep from * to last st. 2 hdc in last hdc. Join with sl st to first hdc. 36 hdc.

17th rnd: As 3rd rnd.

18th rnd: Ch 2. 1 hdc in each of first 8 hdc. *2 hdc in next hdc. 1 hdc in each of next 8 hdc. Rep from * to last st. 2 hdc in last hdc. Join with sl st to first hdc. 40 hdc.

19th rnd: As 3rd rnd.

20th rnd: Ch 2. 1 hdc in each of first 9 hdc. *2 hdc in next hdc. 1 hdc in each of next 9 hdc. Rep from * to last st. 2 hdc in last hdc. Join with sl st to first hdc. 44 hdc.

21st rnd: As 3rd rnd.

22nd rnd: Ch 2. 1 hdc in each of first 10 hdc. *2 hdc in next hdc. 1 hdc in each of next 10 hdc. Rep from * to last st. 2 hdc in last hdc. Join with sl st to first hdc. 48 hdc. Break B.

23rd rnd: Join A. With A, ch 2. *Working in back loops only,* 1 hdc in each hdc around. Join with sl st to first hdc.

24th rnd: Ch 2. 1 hdc in each of first 10 hdc. *Hdc2tog. 1 hdc in each of next 10 hdc. Rep from * to last 2 sts. Hdc2tog. Join with sl st to first hdc. 44 sts.

25th rnd: Ch 2. 1 hdc in each of first 9 hdc. *Hdc2tog. 1 hdc in each of next 9 hdc. Rep from * to last 2 sts. Hdc2tog. Join with sl st to first hdc. 40 sts.

26th rnd: Ch 2. 1 hdc in each of first 2 hdc. *Hdc2tog. 1 hdc in each of next 2 hdc. Rep from * to last 2 hdc. Hdc2tog. Join with sl st to first hdc. 30 sts. Stuff Hand Roll.

27th rnd: Ch 2. 1 hdc in first hdc. *Hdc2tog. 1 hdc in next hdc. Rep from * to last 2 sts. Hdc2tog. Join with sl st to first hdc. 20 sts.

28th rnd: Ch 2. (Hdc2tog) 10 times. Join with sl st to first hdc. 10 sts.

Fasten off leaving a long end. Draw end tightly through rem sts and fasten securely.

Cucumber

With E, ch 10.

1st row: 1 sc in 2nd ch from hook. *Ch 5. 1 sc in next ch. Rep from * to end of chain.

Fasten off.

Salmon (make 2)

With C, ch 3.

1st row: 5 hdc in 3rd ch from hook. Turn.

2nd row: Ch 2. 2 hdc in first hdc. 1 hdc in each hdc to end of row.

Fasten off.

Carrot

With D, ch 6.

1st row: 1 sc in 2nd ch from hook. 1 sc in each ch to end of chain. Turn. 5 sc.

2nd to 4th rows: Ch 1. 1 sc in each sc to end of row. Turn.

Fasten off.

FINISHING

Sew Avocado, Salmon, and Carrot to top of Hand Roll.

With A, stitch on mouth and eyebrows to Maki Roll and Hand Roll using the straight stitch, as seen in the photo. Stitch on eyes using the satin stitch.

With B, stitch on mouth and eyebrows to Sushi Nigiri using the straight stitch, as seen in the photo. Stitch on eyes using the satin stitch. •

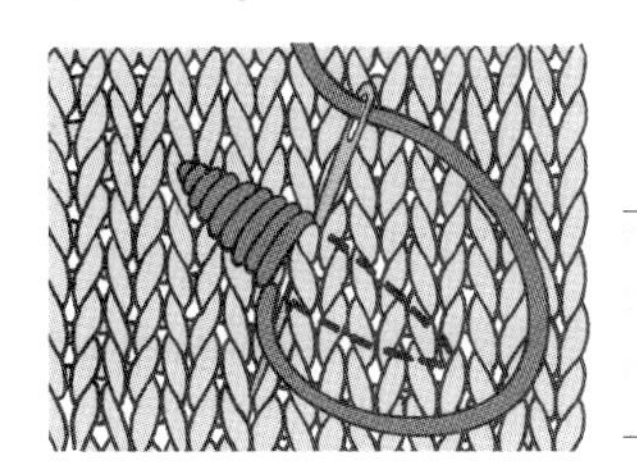

SATIN STITCH

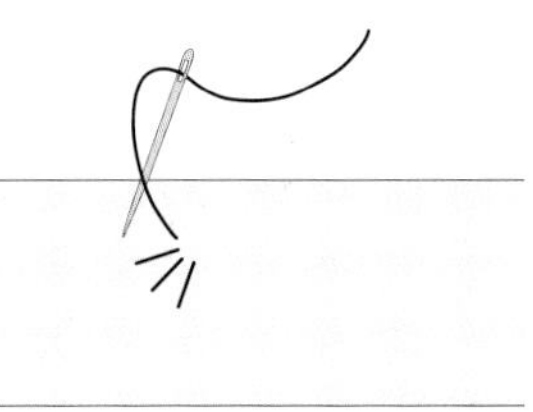

STRAIGHT STITCH

SQUARE HARE

MEASUREMENTS

Approx 6½"/16.5cm long, excluding legs.

MATERIALS

Yarn (4)

Bernat® *Baby Velvet*™, 10½oz/300g balls, each approx 492yd/450m (polyester)

- 1 ball #86018 Cuddly Cloud (A)
- 1 ball in #86005 Orchid Hush (B)

Note: 1 ball each of A and B makes 9 Hares.

Hook

- Size E/4 (3.5mm) crochet hook, *or size needed to obtain gauge*

Notions

- Stuffing
- Pair of 6 mm safety eyes
- Pink embroidery floss

GAUGE

16 sc and 18 rows = 4"/10cm using size E/4 hook.

TAKE TIME TO CHECK GAUGE.

STITCH GLOSSARY

Dcbp Yoh and draw up a loop around post of next stitch at back of work, inserting hook from right to left. (Yoh and draw through 2 loops on hook) twice.

Dcfp Yoh and draw up a loop around post of next stitch at front of work, inserting hook from right to left. (Yoh and draw through 2 loops on hook) twice.

FRONT AND BACK (MAKE 2 ALIKE)

With B, ch 21.

1st row: (RS). 1 sc in 2nd ch from hook. 1 sc in each ch to end of ch. Turn. 20 sc.

2nd row: Ch 1. 1 sc in each sc to end of row. Turn.

Rep last row until piece measures 3 1/2"/9cm, ending on a WS row. Do not fasten off.

Next row: (RS). Ch 2 (counts as hdc). *Dcfp around next sc. Dcbp around next sc. Rep from * to last sc. 1 hdc in last sc. Turn.

Next row: Ch 2 (counts as hdc). *Dcfp around next st. Dcbp around next st. Rep from * to last hdc. 1 hdc in top of ch 2. Break B, join A.

Head

1st row: With A, ch 1. *Working in back loops only,* 1 sc in each st to end of row. Turn.

2nd to 6th rows: Ch 1. 1 sc in each sc to end of row. Turn.

Shape Head

Next row: Ch 1. Sc2tog. 1 sc in each sc to last 2 sc. Sc2tog. Turn. 18 sts.

Rep last row, dec 2 sts every row to 8 sts.

Fasten off.

ARMS (MAKE 2)

**With A, ch 2.

1st rnd: 8 sc in 2nd ch from hook. Join with sl st to first sc.

2nd rnd: Ch 1. 2 sc in each sc around. Join with sl st to first sc. 16 sc.

3rd to 5th rnds: Ch 1. 1 sc in each sc around. Join with sl st to first sc.**

6th rnd: Ch 1. *Sc2tog. 1 sc in each of next 2 sc. Rep from * around. Break A, join B with sl st to first st. 12 sts.

SQUARE HARE

7th rnd: With B, ch 1. 1 sc in each st around. Join with sl st to first sc.

8th rnd: Ch 1. 1 sc in each sc around. Join with sl st to first sc.

Rep last rnd 6 times more, stu¬ffing very lightly (to maintain floppiness of limbs) as you work.

Fasten off at end of last rnd.

LEGS (MAKE 2)

Work from ** to ** as given for Arms.

6th rnd: Ch 1. *Sc2tog. 1 sc in each of next 2 sc. Rep from * around. Join with sl st to first st. 12 sts.

7th rnd: Ch 1. 1 sc in each st around. Join with sl st to first sc.

Rep last rnd 7 times more, stu¬ffing very lightly as you work.

Fasten o at end of last rnd.

EARS (MAKE 2)

With A, ch 10. Join with sl st to first ch.

1st rnd: Ch 1. 1 sc in each ch around. Join with sl st to first sc.

2nd rnd: Ch 1. 1 sc in each of next 4 sc. 2 sc in next sc. 1 sc in each sc to last sc. 2 sc in last sc. Join with sl st to first sc. 12 sc.

3rd rnd: Ch 1. 1 sc in each sc around. Join with sl st to first sc.

4th rnd: Ch 1. 1 sc in each of next 5 sc. 2 sc in next sc. 1 sc in each sc to last sc. 2 sc in last sc. Join with sl st to first sc. 14 sc.

5th to 13th rnds: 1 sc in each sc around. Join with sl st to first sc.

14th rnd: Ch 1. (Sc2tog. 1 sc in each of next 5 sc) twice. 12 sts.

15th rnd: Ch 1. (Sc2tog) 6 times. 6 sts.

Fasten off, leaving long end. Thread end through rem sts and draw up tightly. Fasten securely.

FINISHING

Mark position of Eyes on Front piece. Insert Safety Eyes following manufacturer's instructions. With pink embroidery floss, embroider nose and mouth using satin stitch. With WS of Front and Back tog, sew edges tog, leaving opening for stu¬ffing. Stuff Body. Sew rem edge closed. Attach Arms and Legs. Sew Ears to top of Head. •

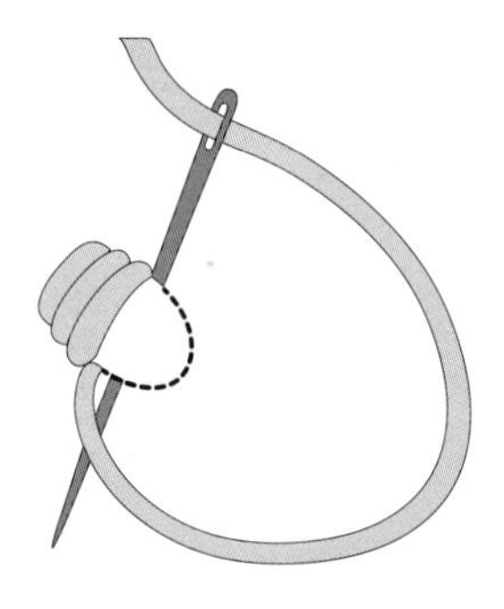

SATIN STITCH

RAINBOW AND SUNSHINE PILLOWS

Easy

RAINBOW PILLOW

MEASUREMENTS

Approx 18"/45.5cm wide

MATERIALS

Yarn

Bernat® *Baby Blanket™*, 3½oz/100g balls, each approx 72yd/65m (polyester)

- 1 ball in #03202 Baby Blue (A)
- 1 ball in #03736 Seafoam (B)
- 1 ball in #03615 Baby Yellow (C)
- 1 ball in #03200 Baby Pink (D)
- 1 ball in #03512 Baby Peach (E)

Hook

- Size L/11 (8mm) crochet hook, *or size needed to obtain gauge*

Notion

- Stuffing

GAUGE

7 sc and 8 rows = 4"/10cm using size L/11 (8mm) crochet hook.

TAKE TIME TO CHECK GAUGE

NOTE

To change color, work to last 2 loops on hook, yoh with new color. Pull through 2 loops on hook to complete st and proceed in new color.

FRONT AND BACK (MAKE 2)

With A, ch 20.

1st row: (RS). 1 sc in 2nd ch from hook. 1 sc in each ch to end of chain. Turn. 19 sts.

2nd row: Ch 1. 1 sc in each sc to end of row. Turn.

3rd row: Ch 1. 1 sc in in each of next 8 sc. 2 sc in each of next 3 sc. 1 sc in each of next 8 sc. Turn. 22 sts.

4th row: Ch 1. 1 sc in each sc to end of row. Turn.

5th row: Ch 1. 1 sc in each of next 8 sc. 2 sc in each of next 6 sc. 1 sc in each of next 8 sc. Join B. Break A. Turn. 28 sts.

6th row: With B, ch 1. 1 sc in each sc to end of row. Turn.

7th row: Ch 1. 1 sc in each of next 8 sc. (2 sc in next sc. 1 sc in next sc) three times. (1 sc in next sc. 2 sc in next sc) 3 times. 1 sc in each of next 8 sc. Turn. 34 sts.

8th row: Ch 1. 1 sc in each sc to end of row. Join C. Break B. Turn.

9th row: With C, ch 1. 1 sc in each of next 8 sc. (2 sc in next sc. 1 sc in each of next 2 sc) 3 times. (1 sc in each of next 2 sc. 2 sc in next sc) 3 times. 1 sc in each of next 8 sc. Turn. 40 sts.

10th row: Ch 1. 1 sc in each sc to end of row. Turn.

11th row: Ch 1. 1 sc in each of next 8 sc. (2 sc in next sc. 1 sc in each of next 3 sc) 3 times. (1 sc in each of next 3 sc. 2 sc in next sc) 3 times. 1 sc in each of next 8 sc. Turn. Break C. Join D. Turn. 46 sts.

12th row: With D, ch 1. 1 sc in each sc to end of row. Turn.

RAINBOW AND SUNSHINE PILLOWS

13th row: Ch 1. 1 sc in each of next 8 sc. (2 sc in next sc. 1 sc in each of next 4 sc) 3 times. (1 sc in each of next 4 sc. 2 sc in next sc) 3 times. 1 sc in each of next 8 sc. Turn. 52 sts.

14th row: Ch 1. 1 sc in each sc to end of row. Join E. Break D. Turn.

15th row: With E, ch 1. 1 sc in each of next 8 sc. (2 sc in next sc. 1 sc in each of next 5 sc) 3 times. (1 sc in each of next 5 sc. 2 sc in next sc) 3 times. 1 sc in each of next 8 sc. Turn. 58 sts.

16th row: Ch 1. 1 sc in each sc to end of row. Turn.

17th row: Ch 1. 1 sc in each of next 8 sc. (2 sc in next sc. 1 sc in each of next 6 sc) 3 times. (1 sc in each of next 6 sc. 2 sc in next sc) 3 times. 1 sc in each of next 8 sc. Turn. 64 sts.

18th to 20th rows: Ch 1. 1 sc in each sc to end of row. Turn. Fasten off.

FINISHING

Seaming

With RS facing, sew Front and Back tog aligning stripes and leaving a small space open for stuffing. Stuff Pillow making sure to shape into a rainbow arc. Sew rem seam.

SUNSHINE PILLOW

MEASUREMENTS

Approx 15"/38cm diameter, including Sun Rays

Yarn (6)

Bernat® *Baby Blanket*™, 3½ oz/100g balls, each approx 72yd/65m (polyester)

- 2 balls in #03615 Baby Yellow

Hook

- Size L/11 (8mm) crochet hook, *or size needed to obtain gauge*

Notions

- Stuffing
- 10yd/9m of worsted weight black yarn for embroidery

GAUGE

7 sc and 8 rows = 4"/10cm using size L/11 (8mm) hook.

TAKE TIME TO CHECK GAUGE.

FRONT AND BACK (MAKE ALIKE)

Ch 2.

1st rnd: 8 sc in 2nd ch from hook. Join with sl st to first sc.

2nd rnd: Ch 1. 2 sc in each sc around. Join with sl st to first sc. 16 sc.

3rd rnd: Ch 1. 1 sc in first sc. 2 sc in next sc. *1 sc in next sc. 2 sc in next sc. Rep from * around. Join with sl st to first sc. 24 sc.

4th rnd: Ch 1. 1 sc in each of first 2 sc. 2 sc in next sc. *1 sc in each of next 2 sc. 2 sc in next sc. Rep from * around. Join with sl st to first sc. 32 sc.

5th rnd: Ch 1. 1 sc in each of first 3 sc. 2 sc in next sc. *1 sc in each of next 3 sc. 2 sc in next sc. Rep from * around. Join with sl st to first sc. 40 sc.

6th to 9th rnds: Cont in same manner, inc 8 sts evenly spaced on every rnd to 72 sc.

Fasten off.

Seaming

With WS of Front and Back facing each other join yarn with sl st through both thicknesses to any sc. Ch 1. Working through both thicknesses, sc in each sc around

leaving a small opening for stu-ffing. Stuff Pillow. Complete rnd of sc to close opening. Join with sl st to first sc. *Do not* fasten off.

Cont as follows for Sun Rays:

First Sun Ray

1st row: Ch 1. 1 sc in each of first 6 sc. Turn. Leave rem sts unworked. 6 sc.

****2nd row:** Ch 1. Skip first sc. 1 sc in each of next 3 sc. Sc2tog. Turn. 4 sc.

3rd row: Ch 1. Skip first sc. 1 sc in next sc. Sc2tog. Turn. 2 sc.

4th row: Ch 1. Sc2tog. Fasten off. **

Second to Twelfth Sun Rays

With RS facing, join yarn with sl st to next skipped sc of joining rnd. Ch 1. 1 sc in same sp as last sl st. 1 sc in each of next 5 sc. Turn. Leave rem sts unworked. 6 sc. Work from ** to ** as given for First Sun Ray.

FINISHING

With black yarn, embroider Eyes and Mouth using chain stitch, using diagram as guide. •

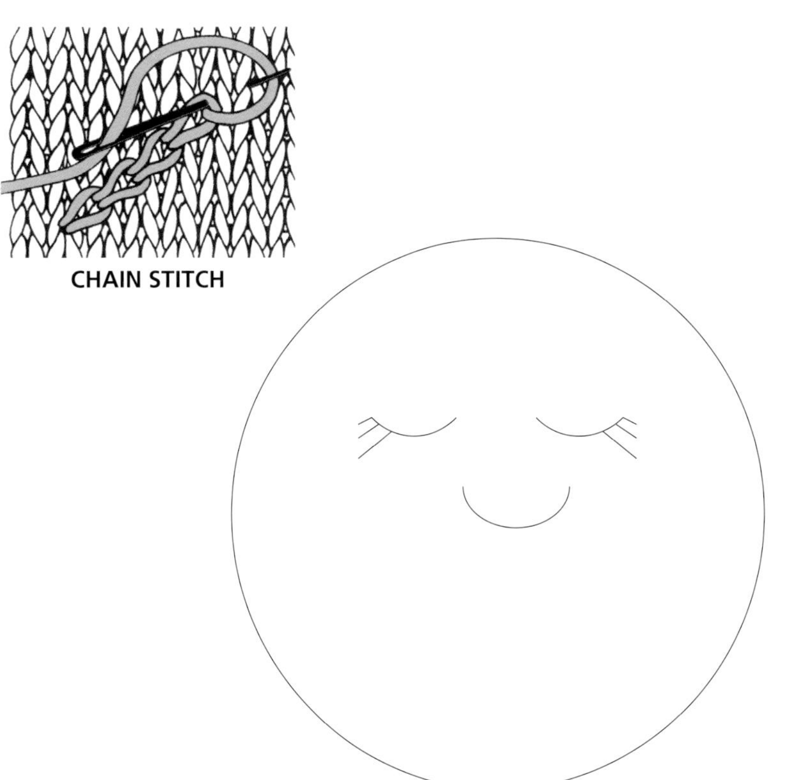

FLYING HEARTS MOBILE

Easy

MATERIALS

Yarn (4)

Red Heart® *Soft Yarn®*, 5oz/141g balls, each approx 256yd/234m (acrylic)

- 1 ball in #2515 Turquoise (A)
- 1 ball in #4422 Tangerine (B)
- 1 ball in #9779 Berry (C)

Hook

- Size H/8 (5mm) crochet hook, *or size needed to obtain gauge*

Notions

- 10yd/9m spool of ¼"/6mm white satin ribbon
- 10"/25cm embroidery hoop
- Yarn needle

GAUGE

17 sc and 16 rows = 4"/10cm using size H/8 (5mm) hook.

TAKE TIME TO CHECK GAUGE.

NOTE

Directions are given for small heart half. Changes for large heart half are in parentheses.

HEART HALF

(Make 6 small heart halves each in A, B and C; make 4 large heart halves each in A, B and C)

Ch 11 (17).

1st rnd: 3 sc in 2nd ch from hook, sc in each of next 3 (6) ch, skip next 2 ch, sc in each of next 3 (6) ch, 3 sc in last ch, working across opposite side of foundation ch, sc in each of next 3 (6) ch, (sc, ch 2, sc) in next ch-2 space, sc in each of next 3 (6) ch.

Do not join rounds, Work in a spiral, marking first st of each round, moving marker up as work progresses.

2nd rnd: 2 sc in each of next 3 sc, sc in each of next 2 (5) sc, skip next 2 sc, sc in each of next 2 (5) sc, 2 sc in each of next 3 sc, sc in each of next 4 (7) sc, (sc, ch 2, sc) in next ch-2 space, sc in each of next 4 (7) sc.

3rd rnd: [2 sc in next sc, sc in next sc] 3 times, sc in each of next 1 (4) sc, skip next 2 sc, sc in each of next 1 (4) sc, [2 sc in next sc, sc in next sc] 3 times, sc in each of next 4 (7) sc, (sc, ch 2, sc) in next ch-2 space, sc in each of next 5 (8) sc.

For small heart, join with slip st in next sc and fasten off

Large Heart Only

4th rnd: Sc in next sc, [2 sc in next sc, sc in next 2 sc] 3 times, sc in each of next 2 sc, skip next 2 sc, sc in each of next 4 sc, [2 sc in next sc, sc in next 2 sc] 3 times, sc in each of next 8 sc, (sc, ch 2, sc) in next ch-2 space, sc in each of next 9 sc.

5th rnd: Sc in next 2 sc, [2 sc in next sc, sc in next 3 sc] 3 times, skip next 2 sc, sc in each of next 3 sc, [2 sc in next sc, sc in next 3 sc] 3 times, sc in each of next 9 sc, (sc, ch 2, sc) in next ch-2 space, sc in each of next 10 sc; join with slip st in next sc.

Fasten off.

FINISHING

Weave in ends.

With wrong sides facing, line up 2 matching heart halves. Using matching yarn, slip st around edge through both hearts, stuff lightly when 2"/5cm from the end.

Repeat for all hearts.

Lay out hearts in groupings—6 groupings with either 2 or 3 hearts, arrange colors as desired. Cut a 24"/60cm

length of ribbon. Tie an overhand knot in ribbon 1"/2.5cm from end, tie a second knot on top of first knot. Put ribbon onto yarn needle, insert needle into a heart from bottom to top, slide heart to knot. Decide position for next heart, tie another knot for base of heart, thread heart onto ribbon. Tie an overhand knot 1"/2.5cm from end of each ribbon. Repeat for each grouping.

Cut two 1yd/1m lengths of ribbon. Fold in half and knot together, about 2"/5cm from fold for a hanging loop.

Open embroidery hoop. Arrange strings of hearts, evenly spaced around hoop. Close embroidery hoop over ends of ribbons.

Tie ends of hanging ribbons, evenly spaced around hoop.

Wrap remaining ribbon around embroidery hoop in a candy cane stripe as pictured. Tie ends to secure. Trim ends. •

NURSERY STORAGE BASKET SET

Easy

MEASUREMENTS

Square

Approx 5½"/14cm × 5½"/14cm × 5½"/14cm

Rectangular

Approx 5½"/14cm × 11"/28cm × 5½"/14cm

MATERIALS

Yarn 

Bernat® *Baby Blanket*™, 10½oz/300g balls, each approx 220yd/201m (polyester)

- 1 ball in #04005 White (A)

Yarn

Bernat® *Baby Velvet*™, 10½oz/300g balls, each approx 492yd/450m (polyester)

- 1 ball in #86016 Misty Gray (B)

Note: 1 ball of A will make 1 Square Basket and 1 Rectangular Basket or 2 Rectangular Baskets or 3 Square Baskets

Hooks

- Size G/6 (4mm) and J/10 (6mm) crochet hooks, *or size needed to obtain gauge*

Notion

- Stitch marker

GAUGES

9 sc and 10 rows = 4"/10cm using size J/10 (6mm) hook with A.

15 sc and 16 rows = 4"/10cm using size G/6 (4mm) hook with B.

TAKE TIME TO CHECK GAUGE.

SQUARE BASKET

With A and larger hook, ch 2.

1st rnd: 8 sc in 2nd ch from hook. Join with sl st to first sc. 8 sc.

2nd rnd: Ch 1. 2 sc in each sc around. Join with sl st to first sc. 16 sc.

3rd rnd: Ch 1. 3 sc in first sc. 1 sc in each of next 3 sc. *3 sc in next sc. 1 sc in each of next 3 sc. Rep from * around. Join with sl st to first sc. 24 sc.

4th rnd: Ch 1. 1 sc in first sc. *3 sc in next sc. 1 sc in each of next 5 sc. Rep from * to last 4 sc. 1 sc in each of last 4 sc. 32 sc.

5th rnd: Ch 1. 1 sc in each of first 2 sc. *3 sc in next sc. 1 sc in each of next 7 sc. Rep from * to last 5 sc. 1 sc in each of last 5 sc. 40 sc.

6th rnd: Ch 1. 1 sc in each of first 3 sc. *3 sc in next sc. 1 sc in each of next 9 sc. Rep from * to last 6 sc. 1 sc in each of last 6 sc. 48 sc.

7th rnd: Ch 1. Working in back loops only, 1 sc in each sc around. Join with sl st to first sc. Place marker.

8th rnd: Ch 1. Working in both loops, 1 sc in each sc around. Join with sl st to first sc. Rep last rnd until Basket from marked rnd measures 5½"/14cm.

Next rnd: Ch 1. Working from left to right instead of right to left as usual, work 1 reverse sc in each sc around. Join with sl st to first sc. Fasten off.

RECTANGULAR BASKET

With A and larger hook, ch 17.

1st rnd: 1 sc in 2nd ch from hook. 1 sc in each of next 14 ch. 3 ch in last ch. Working across opposite side of foundation ch, 1 sc in each of next 14 ch. 2 sc in last ch. Join with sl st to first sc. 34 sc.

2nd rnd: Ch 1. 3 sc in first sc. 1 sc in each of next 14 sc. 3 sc in next sc. 1 sc in next sc. 3 sc in next sc. 1 sc in each

of next 14 sc. 3 sc in next sc. 1 sc in next sc. Join with sl st to first sc. 42 sc.

3rd rnd: Ch 1. 1 sc in first sc. 3 sc in next sc. 1 sc in each of next 16 sc. 3 sc in next sc. 1 sc in each of next 3 sc. 3 sc in next sc. 1 sc in each of next 16 sc. 3 sc in next sc. 1 sc in each of next 2 sc. Join with sl st to first sc. 50 sc.

4th rnd: Ch 1. 1 sc in each of first 2 sc. 3 sc in next sc. 1 sc in each of next 18 sc. 3 sc in next sc. 1 sc in each of next 5 sc. 3 sc in next sc. 1 sc in each of next 18 sc. 3 sc in next sc. 1 sc in each of next 3 sc. Join with sl st to first sc. 58 sc.

5th rnd: Ch 1. 1 sc in each of first 3 sc. 3 sc in next sc. 1 sc in each of next 20 sc. 3 sc in next sc. 1 sc in each of next 7 sc. 3 sc in next sc. 1 sc in each of next 20 sc. 3 sc in next sc. 1 sc in each of next 4 sc. Join with sl st to first sc. 66 sc.

6th rnd: Ch 1. 1 sc in each of first 4 sc. 3 sc in next sc. 1 sc in each of next 22 sc. 3 sc in next sc. 1 sc in each of next 9 sc. 3 sc in next sc. 1 sc in each of next 22 sc. 3 sc in next sc. 1 sc in each of next 5 sc. Join with sl st to first sc. 74 sc.

7th rnd: Ch 1. Working in back loops only, 1 sc in each sc around. Join with sl st to first sc. Place marker.

8th rnd: Ch 1. Working in both loops, 1 sc in each sc around. Join with sl st to first sc. Rep last rnd until Basket from marked rnd measures 5½"/14cm.

Next rnd: Ch 1. Working from left to right instead of right to left as usual, work 1 reverse sc in each sc around. Join with sl st to first sc. Fasten off.

STAR APPLIQUÉ (MAKE 1 PER BASKET)

With B and smaller hook, ch 4. Join with sl st to first ch to form ring.

1st rnd: Ch 3 (counts as dc). 14 dc in ring. Join with sl st to top of ch 3.

2nd rnd: *Ch 5. 1 sc in 2nd ch from hook. 1 hdc in next ch. 1 dc in next ch. 1 tr in next ch. Skip next 2 dc. Sl st in next dc. Rep from * around. Fasten off.

FINISHING

Sew Star to Basket as seen in picture. •

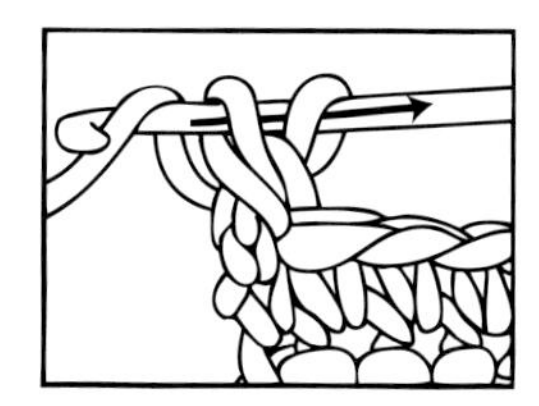

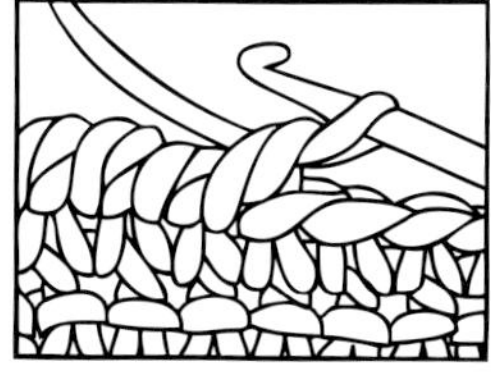

REVERSE SINGLE CROCHET

FAT CAT STUFFIES

Easy

MEASUREMENTS

Approx 10"/25.5cm tall × 9"/23cm diameter

MATERIALS

VERSION 1

Yarn

Bernat® *Baby Crushed Velvet™,* 10½oz/300g balls; each approx 492yd/450m (polyester)

- 1 ball in #13001 Rose Petals (A)
- 1 ball in #86018 Cuddly Cloud (B)

VERSION 2

Yarn

Bernat® *Baby Velvet™,* 10½oz/300g balls, each approx 492yd/450m (polyester)

- 1 ball in #86018 Cuddly Cloud (A)

Yarn 

Bernat® *Baby Crushed Velvet™,* 10½oz/300g balls; each approx 492yd/450m (polyester)

- 1 ball in #13014 Gray Mist (B)

Hook

- Size D/3 (3.25mm) crochet hook, *or size needed to obtain gauge*

Notions

- Stuffing
- 2 stitch markers
- Small amount of Bernat® *Baby Velvet™,* in #86029 Potpourri and #86041 Yolk Yellow for Eyes and Nose
- Small amount of black worsted-weight yarn for eyes and mouth

GAUGE

18 sc and 20 rows = 4"/10cm using size D/3 (3.25mm) hook.

TAKE TIME TO CHECK GAUGE.

NOTES

- Stuffie is worked in a continuous spiral. *Do not* join at end of rnds. Place marker on first stitch of rnd and move marker each rnd to keep place.
- To change colors, work to last 2 loops on hook and draw new color through last 2 loops and proceed.
- When working with 2 colors in one rnd, carry color not in use loosely across top of row and work sts around it.

BODY

With A, ch 2.

1st rnd: 8 sc in 2nd ch from hook, placing marker on first st for beg of rnd. Do not join. 8 sc.

2nd rnd: 2 sc in each sc around. 16 sc.

3rd rnd: *2 sc in next sc. 1 sc in next sc. Rep from * around. 24 sc.

4th rnd: *2 sc in next sc. 1 sc in each of next 2 sc. Rep from * around. 32 sc.

5th rnd: *2 sc in next sc. 1 sc in each of next 3 sc. Rep from * around. 40 sc.

6th rnd: *1 sc in each of next 2 sc. 2 sc in next sc. 1 sc in each of next 2 sc. Rep from * around. 48 sc.

7th rnd: *2 sc in next sc. 1 sc in each of next 5 sc. Rep from * around. 56 sc.

8th rnd: *1 sc in each of next 3 sc. 2 sc in next sc. 1 sc in each of next 3 sc. Rep from * around. 64 sc.

9th rnd: *2 sc in next sc. 1 sc in each of next 7 sc. Rep from * around. 72 sc.

10th rnd: 1 sc in each sc around.

11th rnd: *1 sc in each of next 4 sc. 2 sc in next sc. 1 sc

in each of next 4 sc. Rep from * around. 80 sc.

12th rnd: *2 sc in first sc. 1 sc in each of next 9 sc. Rep from * around. 88 sc.

13th rnd: 1 sc in each sc around.

14th rnd: *1 sc in each of next 5 sc. 2 sc in next sc. 1 sc in each of next 5 sc. Rep from * around. 96 sc.

15th rnd: *2 sc in first sc. 1 sc in each of next 11 sc. Rep from * around. 104 sc.

16th rnd: 1 sc in each sc around.

17th rnd: *1 sc in each of next 6 sc. 2 sc in next sc. 1 sc in each of next 6 sc. Rep from * around. 112 sc.

18th rnd: *2 sc in first sc. 1 sc in each of next 13 sc. Rep from * around. 120 sc.

19th rnd: 1 sc in each sc around. Place 2nd marker at end of rnd—*do not* move 2nd marker each rnd. Rep last rnd until work from 2nd marker measures 4"/10cm.

Proceed as follows:

Next rnd: *Sc2tog. 1 sc in each of next 13 sc. Rep from * around. 112 sc.

Work 3 rnds even in sc.

Next rnd: *Sc2tog. 1 sc in each of next 12 sc. Rep from * around. 104 sc.

Work 1 rnd even in sc.

Shape Face and Head

1st rnd: With A, 1 sc in each of next 16 sc. With B, 1 sc in each sc to end of rnd.

2nd rnd: With B, 1 sc in each of next 2 sc. With A, 1 sc in each of next 12 sc. With B, 1 sc in each sc to end of rnd.

3rd rnd: With B, sc2tog. With A, 1 sc in each of next 11 sc. *With B, sc2tog. With B, 1 sc in each of next 11 sc. Rep from * to end of rnd. 96 sc.

4th rnd: With B, 1 sc in each of next 4 sc. With A, 1 sc in each of next 7 sc. With B, 1 sc in each sc to end of rnd.

5th rnd: With B, 1 sc in each of next 5 sc. With A,

FAT CAT STUFFIES

1 sc in each of next 4 sc. With B, 1 sc in each sc to end of rnd.

6th rnd: With B, sc2tog. With B, 1 sc in each of next 3 sc. With A, 1 sc in each of next 4 sc. With B, 1 sc in each of next 3 sc. *With B, sc2tog. With B, 1 sc in each of next 10 sc. Rep from * to end of rnd. 88 sc.

7th rnd: With B, 1 sc in each of next 6 sc. With A, 1 sc in each of next 3 sc. With B, 1 sc in each sc to end of rnd.

8th rnd: With B, 1 sc in each of next 7 sc. With A, sc2tog. Break A. With B, 1 sc in each of next 3 sc. *With B, sc2tog. With B, 1 sc in each of next 9 sc. Rep from * to end of rnd, ending last rep with 1 sc in each of last 8 sc. 80 sc.

Cont with B only:

9th rnd: 1 sc in each sc around.

10th rnd: *1 sc in each of next 4 sc. Sc2tog. 1 sc in each of next 4 sc. Rep from * around. 72 sc.

11th rnd: 1 sc in each sc around.

12th rnd: *Sc2tog. 1 sc in each of next 7 sc. Rep from * around. 64 sc.

13th rnd: 1 sc in each sc around.

14th rnd: *1 sc in each of next 3 sc. Sc2tog. 1 sc in each of next 3 sc. Rep from * around. 56 sc.

15th rnd: 1 sc in each sc around.

16th rnd: *Sc2tog. 1 sc in each of next 5 sc. Rep from * around. 48 sc.

17th rnd: 1 sc in each sc around.

18th rnd: *1 sc in each of next 2 sc. Sc2tog. 1 sc in each of next 2 sc. Rep from * around. 40 sc. Stuff Body and Head.

19th rnd: 1 sc in each sc around.

20th rnd: *Sc2tog. 1 sc in each of next 3 sc. Rep from * around. 32 sc.

21st rnd: *1 sc in next sc. Sc2tog. 1 sc in next sc. Rep from * around. 24 sc.

22nd rnd: *Sc2tog. 1 sc in next sc. Rep from * around. 16 sc.

23rd rnd: *Sc2tog. Rep from * around. 8 sc.

Fasten off leaving a long end. Thread end through rem sts and fasten securely.

EARS (MAKE 2 EACH WITH A AND B)

Ch 10.

1st row: (RS). 1 sc in 2nd ch from hook. 1 sc in each ch to end of chain. 9 sc. Turn.

2nd and alt rows: Ch 1. 1 sc in each sc to end of row. Turn.

3rd row: Ch 1. Sc2tog. 1 sc in each of next 5 sc. Sc2tog. 7 sc. Turn.

4th row: Ch 1. Sc2tog. 1 sc in each of next 3 sc. Sc2tog. 5 sc. Turn.

5th row: Ch 1. Sc2tog. 1 sc in next sc. Sc2tog. 3 sc. Turn.

6th row: Ch 1. Sc3tog. Fasten off.

VERSION 1

VERSION 2

Join Ears

Hold one A Ear and one B Ear tog with WS facing each other. With A side facing, join B with sl st through both thicknesses to bottom right corner of Ears.

1st row: (RS). Ch 1. Work 8 sc evenly up right side of Ear to corner. 3 sc in corner. Work 8 sc evenly down left side of Ear. Fasten off.

TAIL

With A, ch 2.

Working in spiral as for Body, proceed as follows:

1st rnd: 8 sc in 2nd ch from hook placing marker on first st for beg of rnd. Do not join. 8 sc.

2nd rnd: 2 sc in each sc around. 16 sc.

3rd rnd: *2 sc in next sc. 1 sc in next sc. Rep from * around. 24 sc.

4th to 7th rnds: 1 sc in each sc around, joining B at end of 7th rnd.

Break A.

8th rnd: *With B, sc2tog. 1 sc in next sc. Rep from * around. 16 sc.

9th rnd: 1 sc in each sc around.

Rep last rnd until Tail from beg measures 7"/18cm. Fasten off.

HANDS (MAKE 2)

With A, ch 5.

Working in spiral as for Body, proceed as follows:

1st rnd: 1 sc in 2nd ch from hook. Place marker on last st for beg of rnd. 1 sc in each of next 2 ch. 3 sc in last ch. *Working across opposite side of foundation ch,* 1 sc in each of next 2 ch. 2 sc in last ch. Do not join. 10 sc.

2nd rnd: 1 sc in each of first 4 sc. 3 sc in next sc. 1 sc in each of next 4 sc. 3 sc in last sc. 14 sc.

3rd to 6th rnds: 1 sc in each sc around, joining B at end of last rnd.

8th to 10th rnds: With B, 1 sc in each sc around. Fasten off.

FEET (MAKE 2)

With A, ch 2.

Working in spiral as for Body, proceed as follows:

1st rnd: 8 sc in 2nd ch from hook placing marker on first st for beg of rnd. Do not join. 8 sc.

2nd rnd: 2 sc in each sc around. 16 sc.

3rd rnd: 1 sc in first sc. 2 hdc in next sc. (2 dc in next dc. 1 dc in next dc) twice. 2 dc in next sc. 2 hdc in next sc. (1 sc in next sc. 2 sc in next sc) 4 times. 25 sts.

4th rnd: *Working in back loops only,* 1 sc in each st to end of rnd.

5th and 6th rnds: *Working in both loops,* 1 sc in each sc to end of rnd.

7th rnd: 1 sc in first sc sc. (Sc2tog) twice. 1 sc in next sc. Sc2tog. 1 sc in next sc. (Sc2tog) twice. 1 sc in each sc to end of rnd. 20 sc.

8th rnd: *Sc2tog. 1 sc in each of next 2 sc. Rep from * around. 15 sc.

9th to 12th rnds: 1 sc in each sc around. Fasten off.

EYES (MAKE 2).

With black yarn, ch 2.

1st rnd: 8 sc in 2nd ch from hook. Join with sl st to first sc. Fasten off. Join Yolk Yellow yarn with sl st to any sc.

2nd rnd: Ch 1. 2 sc in each sc around. Join with sl st to first sc. Fasten off.

FINISHING

Stuff Tail, Hands and Feet and sew to Body as seen in picture. Sew Ears to top of Head as seen in picture. Sew Eyes to Head as seen in picture. With Potpourri yarn, embroider nose with satin stitch as seen in picture. With black yarn, embroider mouth with straight stitch as seen in picture. •

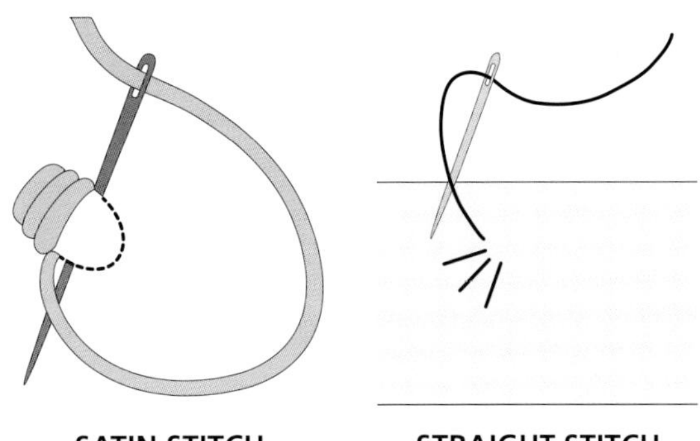

SATIN STITCH　　STRAIGHT STITCH

HEART PILLOW

Easy

MEASUREMENTS

Approx 8"/45.4cm × 19"/48.5cm

MATERIALS

Yarn 

Bernat® *Baby Velvet™*, 10½oz/300g balls, each approx 492yd/450m (polyester)

- 1 ball #86013 Pink Mist

Hook

- Size H/8 (5mm) crochet hook, *or size needed to obtain gauge*

Notions

- Stitch markers
- Stuffing

GAUGE

13 sc and 14 rows = 4"/10cm using size H/8 (5mm) hook.

TAKE TIME TO CHECK GAUGE.

FRONT AND BACK (MAKE 2)

Ch 2.

1st row: (WS). 3 sc in 2nd ch from hook. Turn.

2nd row: Ch 1. 1 sc in first sc. 2 sc in next sc. 1 sc in next sc. Turn. 4 sc.

3rd row: Ch 1. 1 sc in first sc. 2 sc in each of next 2 sc. 1 sc in next sc. Turn. 6 sc.

4th to 6th rows: Ch 1. 1 sc in each of first 2 sc. 2 sc in next sc. 1 sc in each sc to last 3 sc. 2 sc in next sc. 1 sc in each of last 2 sc. Turn.

7th row: (WS). Ch 1. 1 sc in each sc to end of row. Turn. Rep 4th to 7th rows 6 times more. more. 48 sc.

Next row: (RS). Ch 1. 1 sc in each of first 2 sc. 2 sc in next sc. 1 sc in each sc to last 3 sc. 2 sc in next sc. 1 sc in each of last 2 sc. Turn. 50 sc.

Next row: (WS). Ch 1. 1 sc in each sc to end of row. Turn. Rep these 2 rows 6 times more. 62 sc.

Next row: Ch 1. 1 sc in each sc to end of row. Turn. Rep last row until work from beg measures 13"/33cm, ending on a WS row.

Right Side Shaping

****1st row: (RS).** Ch 1. 1 sc in each of first 2 sc. Sc2tog. 1 sc in each of next 23 sc. Sc2tog. 1 sc in each of next 2 sc. Place marker on next st. Turn. 29 sc.

2nd and alt rows: Ch 1. 1 sc in each sc to end of row. Turn.

3rd row: Ch 1. 1 sc in each of first 2 sc. Sc2tog. 1 sc in each of next 21 sc. Sc2tog. 1 sc in each of next 2 sc. Turn. 27 sc.

5th, 7th, 9th, 11th and 13th rows: Ch 1. 1 sc in each of first 2 sc. Sc2tog. 1 sc in each sc to last 4 sc. Sc2tog. 1 sc in each of last 2 sc. Turn. 17 sc at end of 13th row.

15th row: Ch 1. 1 sc in each of first 2 sc. Sc3tog. 1 sc in each of next 7 sc. Sc3tog. 1 sc in each of last 2 sc. Turn. 13 sc.

17th row: Ch 1. 1 sc in each of first 2 sc. Sc3tog. 1 sc in each of next 3 sc. Sc3tog. 1 sc in each of last 2 sc. 9 sc.

19th row: Ch 1. Sc3tog. 1 sc in each of next 3 sc. Sc3tog. Fasten off.**

Left Side Shaping

Join yarn with sl st to marked st. Work from ** to ** as given for Right Side Shaping, beg in same st as last sl st.

FINISHING

Place WS of Back and Front facing each other. With RS of Front facing and working *through both thicknesses,* join yarn with sl st to bottom point, and work in sc around outer edge of Pillow, stuffing Pillow before rnd is complete. Join with sl st to first sc.

Fasten off. •

PREEMIE OCTOPUS

Easy

MEASUREMENTS
Approx 12"/30.5cm long, including tentacles

MATERIALS
Yarn 

Red Heart® *Bunches of Hugs®*, 14oz/397g balls, each approx 948yd/868m (acrylic)

- 1 ball in #5514 Capri

Note: 1 ball will make 5 Preemie Octopus toys.

Hook
- Size G/6 (4mm) crochet hook, *or size needed to obtain gauge*

Notions
- Stitch markers
- Stuffing
- Black embroidery floss for eyes and mouth

GAUGE
15 sc and 18 rows = 4"/10cm using size G/6 (4mm) hook.

TAKE TIME TO CHECK GAUGE.

NOTE
Head of Octopus is worked in continuous rnds. Do not join at end of rnds. Place a st marker to indicate beg of rnds and move marker as each rnd is worked.

HEAD
Ch 2.

****1st rnd:** 7 sc in 2nd ch from hook. 7 sc.

2nd rnd: 2 sc in each sc around. 14 sc.

3rd rnd: *1 sc in next sc. 2 sc in next sc. Rep from * around. 21 sc.

4th rnd: *1 sc in each of next 2 sc. 2 sc in next sc. Rep from * around. 28 sc.

5th rnd: *1 sc in each of next 3 sc. 2 sc in next sc. Rep from * around. 35 sc.

6th and 7th rnds: 1 sc in each sc around.

8th rnd: *1 sc in each of next 4 sc. 2 sc in next sc. Rep from * around. 42 sc.

9th and 10th rnds: 1 sc in each sc around.

11th rnd: *1 sc in each of next 5 sc. 2 sc in next sc. Rep from * around. 49 sc.

12th and 13th rnds: 1 sc in each sc around.

14th rnd: *1 sc in each of next 6 sc. 2 sc in next sc. Rep from * around. 56 sc.

15th to 20th rnds: 1 sc in each sc around.

21st rnd: *1 sc in each of next 6 sc. Sc2tog. Rep from * around. 49 sts.

22nd rnd: 1 sc in each sc around.

23rd rnd: *1 sc in each of next 5 sc. Sc2tog. Rep from * around. 42 sts.

24th rnd: 1 sc in each sc around.

25th rnd: *1 sc in each of next 4 sc. Sc2tog. Rep from * around. 35 sts.

26th rnds: 1 sc in each sc around.

27th rnd: 1 sc in each of rst 3 sc. *Sc2tog. 1 sc in each of next 9 sc. Rep from * around. 32 sts.

28th rnd: *Working in back loops only,* 1 sc in each sc around. Place a marker on last rnd.

29th rnd: *Working in both loops,* *1 sc in each of next 2 sc. Sc2tog. Rep from * around. 24 sts. Stuff Head.

30th rnd: Ch 1. *1 sc in next sc. Sc2tog. Rep from * around. 16 sts.

31st rnd: Ch 1. *Sc2tog. Rep from * around. 8 sts. Cut yarn, leaving a long end.

Fasten off. Thread end of yarn through rem 8 sts. Pull tightly. Fasten securely.

Divide for 8 Tentacles:

Join yarn with sl st to any rem front loop of marked rnd.

1st Tentacle: Ch 38. 4 dc in 4th ch from hook. *5 dc in next ch. Rep from * to end of chain. Skip next 3 sc of 27th rnd. Sl st in next sc.

2nd to 8th Tentacles: As 1st Tentacle.

FINISHING

Fasten off at end of 8th Tentacle. With black embroidery floss, embroider mouth using straight stitch and eyes, using French knots. •

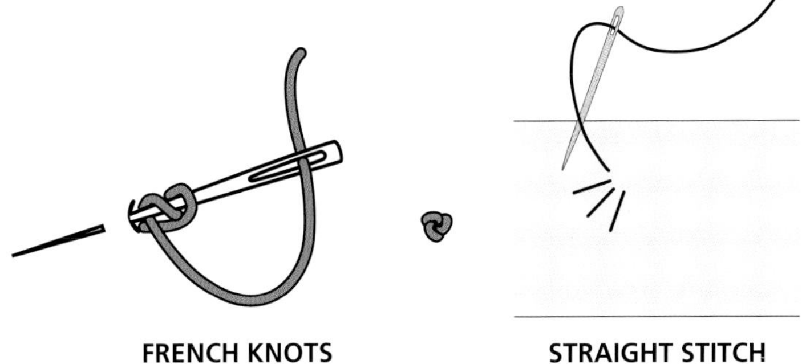

LOOPY LLAMA BLANKET

Intermediate

MEASUREMENTS

Approx 33"/84cm x 38½"/98cm

MATERIALS

Yarn 

Bernat® *Baby Blanket™*, 10½oz/300g balls, each approx 220yd/201m (polyester)

- 2 balls in #04512 Baby Peach (A)
- 2 balls in #04008 Vanilla (B)

Yarn 

Bernat® *Baby Blanket™*, 3½oz/100g balls, each approx 72yd/65m (polyester)

1 ball in #03736 Seafoam (C)

Hook

- Size K/10½ (6.5mm) and L/11 (8mm) crochet hooks, *or size needed to obtain gauge*

Notion

- Small quantity of bulky-weight black yarn for embroidery

GAUGE

7 sc and 8 rows = 4"/10cm using size L/11 (8mm) hook.

TAKE TIME TO CHECK GAUGE.

STITCH GLOSSARY

Lp st = Loop stitch (worked on WS) = Yoh and insert hook in next stitch. Hold working yarn over top of left index finger and pull up 1"/2.5cm loop. Grab working yarn behind index finger and pull through stitch. Hold loop in position with right hand to front of work. Yoh and draw through 3 loops on hook. Loop is formed on RS of work.

NOTE

Color changes are worked in intarsia technique. Wind small balls of colors to be used, one for each separate area of color in the design. Start new colors at appropriate points. Do not carry color not in use along top of work. To join new color, work to last 2 loops on hook of first color. Yoh with new color, draw through loops and proceed with new color.

BLANKET

With C and larger hook, ch 57. See chart on page 51.

1st row: (RS). 1 sc in 2nd ch from hook. 1 sc in each ch to end of ch. Turn. 56 sc.

2nd row: Ch 1. 1 Lp st in each st to end of row. Turn.

3rd row: Ch 1. 1 sc in each st to end of row. Turn.

4th and 5th rows: As 2nd and 3rd rows. Break C. Join A.

6th row: With A, ch 1. 1 sc in each of next 12 sts. With B, 1 Lp st in each st to last 12 sts. With A, 1 sc in each st to end of row. Turn.

7th row: With A, ch 1. 1 sc in each of next 12 sts. With B, 1 sc in each st to last 12 sts. With A, 1 sc in each st to end of row. Turn.

8th to 31st rows: Rep 6th and 7th rows 12 times.

32nd row: With A, ch 1. 1 sc in each of next 12 sts. With B, 1 Lp st in each of next 14 sts. 1 sc in each of next 4 sts. 1 Lp st in each of next 14 sts. With A, 1 sc in each st to end of row. Turn.

33rd and alt rows: As 7th row.

34th row: With A, ch 1. 1 sc in each of next 12 sts. With B, 1 Lp st in each of next 13 sts. 1 sc in each of next 6 sts. 1 Lp st in each of next 13 sts. With A, 1 sc in each st to end of row. Turn.

36th row: With A, ch 1. 1 sc in each of next 12 sts. With B, 1 Lp st in each of next 12 sts. 1 sc in each of next

LOOPY LLAMA BLANKET

8 sts. 1 Lp st in each of next 12 sts. With A, 1 sc in each st to end of row. Turn.

38th row: As 36th row.

40th row: As 34th row.

42nd row: As 32nd row.

43rd row: As 7th row.

44th to 53rd rows: Rep 6th and 7th rows 5 times.

54th row: As 6th row.

55th row: With A, ch 1. 1 sc in each of next 12 sts. *With B, 1 sc in each of next 10 sts. With A, 1 sc in each of next 12 sts. Rep from * to end of row. Turn.

56th row: With A, ch 1. 1 sc in each of next 12 sts. *With B, 1 Lp st in each of next 10 sts. With A, 1 sc in each of next 12 sts. Rep from * to end of row. Turn.

57th and 58th rows: As 55th and 56th rows.

59th row: With A, ch 1. 1 sc in each of next 13 sts. With B, 1 sc in each of next 8 sts. With A, 1 sc in each of next 14 sts. With B, 1 sc in each of next 8 sts. With A, 1 sc in each of next 13 sts. Turn.

60th row: With A, ch 1. 1 sc in each of next 13 sts.

With B, 1 Lp st in each of next 8 sts. With B, 1 sc in each of next 14 sts. With B, 1 Lp st in each of next 8 sts. With A, 1 sc in each of next 13 sts. Turn.

61st and 62nd rows: As 59th and 60th rows.

63rd row: With A, ch 1. 1 sc in each of next 14 sts. With B, 1 sc in each of next 6 sts. With A, 1 sc in each of next 16 sts. With B, 1 sc in each of next 6 sts. With A, 1 sc in each of next 14 sts. Turn.

64th row: With A, ch 1. 1 sc in each of next 14 sts. With B, 1 Lp st in each of next 6 sts. With A, 1 sc in each of next 16 sts. With B, 1 Lp st in each of next 6 sts. With A, 1 sc in each of next 14 sts. Turn.

65th and 66th rows: As 63rd and 64th rows.

67th row: With A, ch 1. 1 sc in each of next 15 sts. With B, 1 sc in each of next 5 sts. With A, 1 sc in each of next 16 sts. With B, 1 sc in each of next 5 sts. With A, 1 sc in each of next 15 sts. Turn.

68th row: With A, ch 1. 1 sc in each of next 15 sts. With B, 1 Lp st in each of next 5 sts. With A, 1 sc in each of next 16 sts. With B, 1 Lp st in each of next 5 sts. With A, 1 sc in each of next 15 sts. Turn.

69th and 70th rows: As 67th and 68th rows.

71st row: With A, ch 1. 1 sc in each of next 16 sts. With B, 1 sc in each of next 4 sts. With A, 1 sc in each of next 16 sts. With B, 1 sc in each of next 4 sts. With A, 1 sc in each of next 16 sts. Turn.

72nd row: With A, ch 1. 1 sc in each of next 16 sts. With B, 1 Lp st in each of next 4 sts. With A, 1 sc in each of next 16 sts. With B, 1 Lp st in each of next 4 sts. With A, 1 sc in each of next 16 sts. Turn.

73rd row: As 71st row.

74th and 75th rows: With A, ch 1. 1 sc in each st to end of row. Turn. Do not fasten off at end of 75th row.

FINISHING

Border

1st rnd: With A, ch 1. 1 sc in each st to end of row. 3 sc in corner. Work 65 sc evenly down left side of Blanket. 3 sc in corner. 1 sc in each rem ch across foundation ch to end of row. 3 sc in corner. Work 65 sc evenly up right side of Blanket. 3 sc in corner. Join with sl st to first sc.

Fasten off.

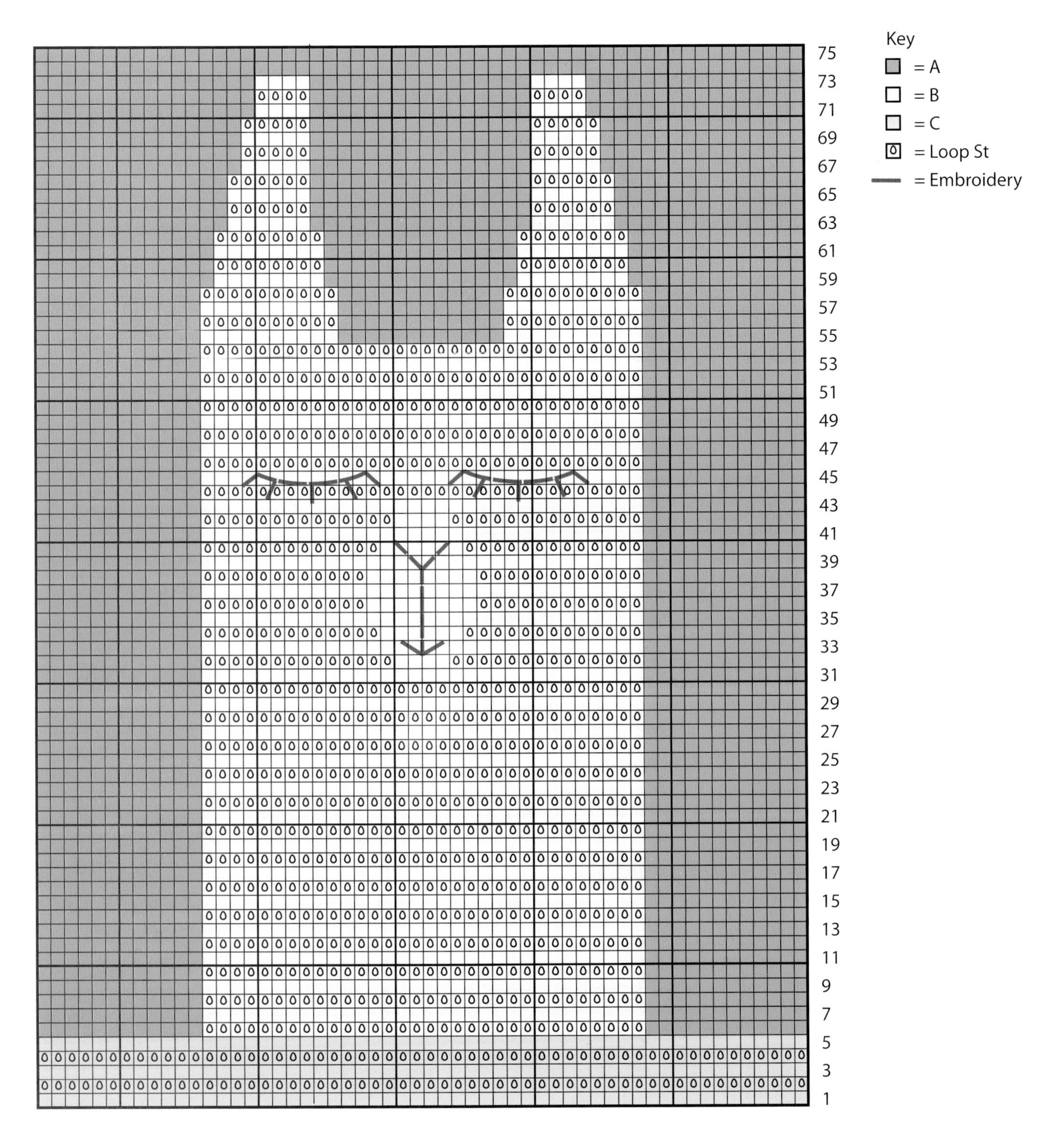

Face

Using black yarn, embroider eyes, nose, and mouth with back stitch (see diagram) as shown on chart. •

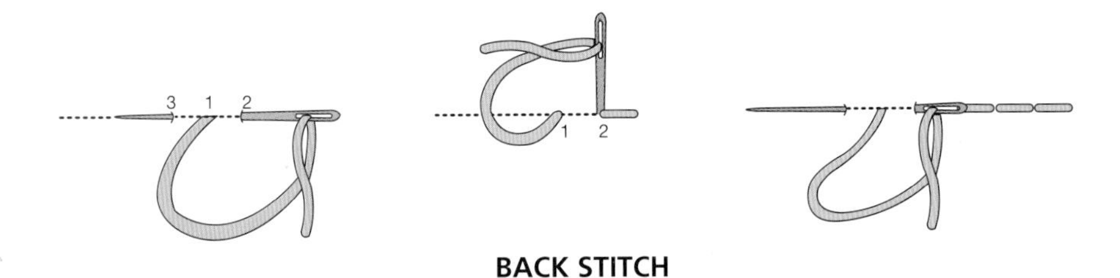

BACK STITCH

SMALL FRY SLEEP SACK

Easy

MEASUREMENTS

Approx 22"/56cm × 32"/81.5cm, including French Fries.

MATERIALS

Yarn 6

Bernat® *Blanket Brights™*, 10½oz/300g balls, each approx 220yd/201m (polyester)

- 2 balls in #12001 Race Car Red (A)
- 1 ball in #12003 School Bus Yellow (B)

Hooks

- Size K/10½ (6.5mm) and size L/11 (8mm) crochet hooks, *or size needed to obtain gauge*

GAUGE

7 sc and 8 rows= 4"/10cm with larger hook.
TAKE TIME TO CHECK GAUGE.

SACK FRONT

**With larger hook and A, ch 29.

1st row: (RS). 1 sc in 2nd ch from hook. 1 sc in each ch across. Turn. 28 sc.

2nd to 7th rows: Ch 1. 1 sc in each sc to end of row. Turn.

8th row: Ch 1. 1 sc in first sc. 2 sc in next sc. 1 sc in each sc to last 2 sc. 2 sc in next sc. 1 sc in last sc. Turn. 30 sc.

Rep 2nd to 8th rows 4 times more. 38 sc.**

Shape Top Right

1st row: (RS). Ch 1. 1 sc in each of first 14 sc. Turn. Leave rem sts unworked.

2nd row: Ch 1. Sc2tog. 1 sc in each sc to end of row. Turn. 13 sc.

3rd row: Ch 1. 1 sc in each sc to last 2 sts. Sc2tog. Turn. 12 sc. Rep 2nd and 3rd rows until 7 sts rem.

Fasten off.

Shape Top Left

With RS facing, skip next 10 sc. Join A with sl st to next sc.

1st row: (RS). Ch 1. 1 sc in same sp as last sl st. 1 sc in each of next 13 sc. Turn.

2nd row: Ch 1. 1 sc in each sc to last 2 sts. Sc2tog. 12 sc.

3rd row: Ch 1. Sc2tog. 1 sc in each sc to end of row. Turn. 13 sc.

Rep 2nd and 3rd rows until 7 sts rem.

Fasten off.

Back Work from ** to ** as given for Front.

Next row: Ch 1. 1 sc in each sc to end of row. Turn.

Rep last row 7 times more.

Shape Top

1st row: Ch 1. Sc2tog. 1 sc in each sc to last 2 sts. Sc2tog. Turn. 36 sc.

Rep 1st row 10 times more. 16 sc.

Fasten off.

FINISHING

With WS of Front and Back facing each other, sew around bottom and sides of Sack.

Top Edging (RS)

Join A with sl st at side seam. Ch 1. *Working from left to right, instead of from right to left as usual,* work 1 reverse sc in each st around top opening of Sack. Join with sl st to first sc.

Fasten off.

FRENCH FRIES

Note: Ch 2 at beg of row does not count as hdc.

Small Fries (make 4)

With smaller hook and B, ch 27.

1st row: 1 hdc in 3rd ch from hook. 1 hdc in each ch across. Turn. 25 hdc.

2nd row: Ch 2. 1 hdc in each st across. Turn.

3rd row: As 2nd row.

Fasten off.

Medium Fries (make 4)

With smaller hook and B, ch 31.

1st row: 1 hdc in 3rd ch from hook. 1 hdc in each ch across. Turn. 29 hdc.

2nd row: Ch 2. 1 hdc in each st across. Turn.

3rd row: As 2nd row.

Fasten off.

Large Fries (make 4)

With smaller hook and B, ch 37.

1st row: 1 hdc in 3rd ch from hook. 1 hdc in each ch across. Turn. 35 hdc.

2nd row: Ch 2. 1 hdc in each st across. Turn.

3rd row: As 2nd row.

Fasten off.

FINISHING

Join Fries

With B and 2 Fries of same size held tog, work 1 sc in each st around outer edge of Fry, through both thicknesses, working 3 sc in each corner. Join with sl st to first sc.

Fasten off.

Sew Fries to Back of Sack as illustrated in this order: Small, Medium, Large, Large, Medium, Small. •

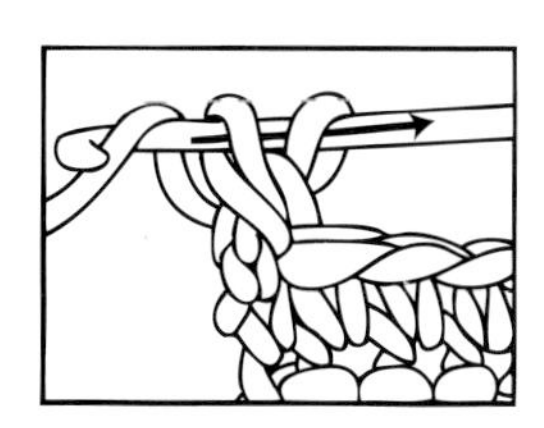

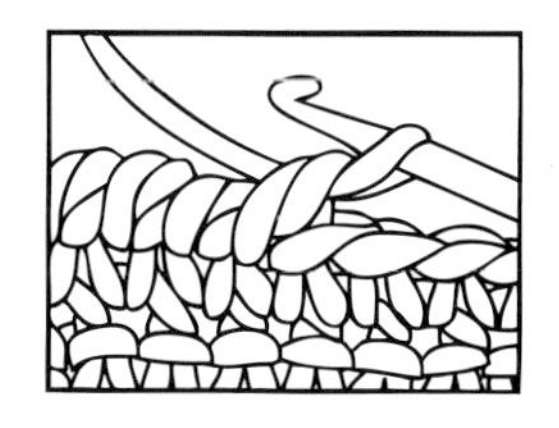

REVERSE SINGLE CROCHET

POMP-A-POODLE

Intermediate

MEASUREMENTS

13"/33cm tall × 12"/30cm from nose to end (excluding tail)

MATERIALS

Yarn 

Red Heart® *Super Saver®*, 7oz/198g balls, each approx 364yd/215m (acrylic)

- 1 ball in #373 Petal Pink (A)
- 1 ball in #316 Soft White (B)
- 1 ball in #312 Black (C)

Yarn 

Red Heart® *Pomp-a-Doodle™*, 3½oz/100g balls, each approx 14yd/13m (polyester)

- 1 ball in #9785 Cotton Candy Pink (D)

Hooks

- Size F/5 (3.75mm) and size H/8 (5mm) crochet hooks, *or size needed to obtain gauge*

Notions

- Yarn needle
- Stitch marker
- Black embroidery floss
- Stuffing
- Strong hand-sewing thread and needle
- Buttons or plastic safety eyes
- Optional ribbon
- Plastic pellets and knee-high hose for making pellet packet.

Notes: Do not use buttons or safety eyes for children under 2 years of age, embroider eyes instead.

GAUGE

20 sc and 16 rnds = 4"/10cm using size size F/5 (3.75mm) hook.

TAKE TIME TO CHECK GAUGE.

NOTES

- Work in continuous rounds without joining.
- Mark beginning of round. Move marker up each round.

HEAD (BEGIN AT NOSE)

1st rnd: With C and smaller hook, ch 2; 6 sc in 2nd ch from hook.

2nd rnd: [Inc] 6 times. 12 sc.

3rd and 4th rnds: Sc in each sc around.

5th rnd: Dec, sc in next 9 sc, slip st in next sc. 11 sts. Fasten off. Stuff with black yarn remnants to prevent stuffing show-through.

6th rnd: Join B in any st; ch 1, [inc, sc in next sc] 5 times, inc. 17 sc.

7th rnd: Sc in each sc around.

8th rnd: Inc, sc in next 8 sc, inc, sc in next 7 sc. 19 sc.

9th rnd: Inc, sc in next 9 sc, inc, sc in next 8 sc. 21 sc.

10th rnd: Inc, sc in next 10 sc, inc, sc in next 9 sc. 23 sc.

11th rnd: Inc, sc in next 11 sc, inc, sc in next 10 sc. 25 sc.

12th rnd: [Inc, sc in next 4 sc] 5 times. 30 sc.

13th rnd: [Inc, sc in next 4 sc] 6 times. 36 sc.

14th rnd: Sc in each sc around.

15th rnd: [Inc, sc in next 5 sc] 6 times. 42 sc.

16th rnd: [Inc, sc in next 6 sc] 6 times. 48 sc.

17th rnd: [Inc, sc in next 7 sc] 6 times. 54 sc.

18th–23rd rnds: Sc in each sc around.

24th rnd: [Inc, sc in next 8 sc] 6 times. 60 sc.

25th rnd: Sc in each sc around.

26th rnd: [Dec, sc in next 4 sc] 10 times. 50 sc.

27th rnd: [Dec, sc in next 3 sc] 10 times. 40 sc.

28th rnd: [Dec, sc in next 2 sc] 10 times. 30 sc. Stuff head firmly, continuing as rounds are worked.

29th rnd: [Dec, sc in next sc] 10 times. 20 sc.

30th rnd: Sc in each sc around. Finish stuffing head.

31st rnd: [Dec] 10 times. 10 sc.

32nd rnd: [Dec] 5 times. 5 sc.

Fasten off, weaving yarn tail through sc to close hole.

POMP-A-POODLE

BODY (BEGINNING AT REAR END)

1st rnd: Using A and smaller hook, ch 2; 6 sc in 2nd ch from hook.

2nd rnd: [Inc] 6 times. 12 sc.

3rd rnd: [Inc, sc in next sc] 6 times. 18 sc.

4th rnd: [Inc, sc in next 2 sc] 6 times. 24 sc.

5th rnd: [Inc, sc in next 3 sc] 6 times. 30 sc.

6th rnd: [Inc, sc in next 4 sc] 6 times. 36 sc.

7th rnd: [Inc, sc in next 5 sc] 6 times. 42 sc.

8th rnd: [inc, sc in next 6 sc] 6 times. 48 sc.

9th rnd: Sc in each sc around.

10th rnd: [Inc, sc in next 7 sc] 6 times. 54 sc.

11th rnd: [Inc, sc in next 8 sc] 6 times. 60 sc.

12th and 13th rnds: Sc in each sc around.

14th rnd: Back Leg Openings: Sc in next 3 sc, ch 8, skip 10 sc, sc in next 2 sc, ch 8, skip 10 sc, sc in next 35 sc. 56 sc.

15th–23rd rnds: Sc in each ch and sc around. 56 sc.

24th rnd: Front Leg Openings: Sc in next 3 sc, ch 8, skip 10 sc, sc in next 2 sc, ch 8, skip 10 sc, sc in next 31 sc. 52 sc.

25th rnd: Inc, sc in next 23 sts, inc, sc in next 27 sc. 54 sc.

26th rnd: Inc, sc in next 24 sts, inc, sc in next 28 sts. 56 sc.

27th rnd: Sc in each sc around.

28th rnd: Neck Opening: Sc in next 39 sc, ch 10, skip 10 sc, sc in next 7 sc. 56 sc.

29th rnd: Sc in each ch and sc around. 56 sc. Stuff poodle body as rounds are worked.

30th rnd: [Sc in next 6 sc, dec] 7 times. 49 sc.

31st rnd: Sc in next sc, [dec, sc in next 4 sc] 8 times. 41 sc.

32nd rnd: Sc in next sc, [dec] 20 times. 21 sc. Continue to stuff body.

33rd rnd: Sc in next sc, [dec] 10 times. 11 sc.

34th rnd: Sc in next sc, [dec] 5 times. 6 sc.

35th rnd: [Dec] 3 times. 3 sc.

Fasten off, weaving yarn tail through sc to close hole.

LEGS (MAKE 4)

1st rnd: Join B to any st in leg opening; ch 1, sc in each ch and sc around inc 3 sts evenly spaced. 21 sc.

2nd–14th rnds: Sc in each sc around, changing to A in the last st of the last round. Fasten off B.

15th rnd: With A, slip st loosely at base of each sc around (this will be the foundation for applying leg pouf).

16th rnd: Sc in each sc of Rnd 14 around. 21 sc. Stuff upper section of leg. If using plastic pellets to add weight to poodle, place about ¼ cup in the toe of a kneehigh stocking, cut and tightly knot. Stuff this into bottommost parts needing extra weight, finish stuffing with polyester filler.

17th rnd: Sc in next sc, [inc, sc in next 4 sc] 4 times. 25 sc.

18th rnd: Sc in each sc around.

19th rnd: [Inc, sc in next 4 sc] 5 times. 30 sc.

20th rnd: [Inc, sc in next 5 sc] 5 times. 35 sc.

21st rnd: [Dec, sc in next 5 sc] 5 times. 30 sc.

22nd rnd: [Dec] 15 times. 15 sc. Finish stuffing.

23rd rnd: [Dec] 7 times, sc in next sc. 8 sc.

24th rnd: [Dec] 4 times. 4 sc.

Fasten off leaving long tail for sewing. Repeat for other legs.

Pomp-a-Doodle yarn is worked in the thread between the pompons. Do not pull pompons through stitches.

Leg Pouf

1st rnd: Join D in any slip st of Round 15; sc in each slip st around leg.

2nd rnd: Sc in each sc around.

Fasten off.

Neck

1st rnd: Attach A to any sc in neck opening; ch 1, sc in each ch and sc around inc 6 sts evenly spaced. 26 sc.

2nd–7th rnds: Sc in each sc around.

Fasten off leaving yarn tail for attaching head.

Ribbed Sweater Collar

1st row: Ch 7; sc in 2nd ch from hook and in each ch across; turn. 6 sc.

2nd–21st rows: Ch 1, sc in back loops only in each sc across; turn.

Fasten off leaving long tail for attaching to neck.

Edging

Join D in end of any row of collar; slip st evenly across row ends (about 12 pompoms).

Fasten off.

TAIL

With smaller hook and A, ch 4; join with a slip st to form a ring.

1st rnd: Ch 1, 6 sc in ring; do not join; work in continuous rounds.

2nd–12th rnds: Work even in sc. Fasten off A in last sc.

13th rnd: Join D in any sc; slip st (1 pompom per slip st) in each sc around.

14th rnd: * 2 Slip sts in next slip st, slip st in next slip st; repeat from * around.

15th rnd: Slip st in every other st around.

Fasten off.

EARS (MAKE 2)

With smaller hook and B, ch 12; join with a slip st to form a ring.

1st rnd: Ch 1, sc in each ch around; do not join. 12 sc.

2nd–6th rnds: Sc in each sc around.

7th rnd: [Inc, sc in next 5 sc] twice. 14 sc.

8th and 9th rnds: Sc in each sc around.

10th rnd: [Inc, sc in next 6 sc] twice. 16 sc.

11th rnd: Sc in each sc around.

12th rnd: [Inc, sc in next 7 sc] twice. 18 sc.

13th rnd: [Inc, sc in next 8 sc] twice. 20 sc.

14th rnd: Sc in each sc around.

15th rnd: [Inc, sc in next 9 sc] twice. 22 sc.

16th and 17th rnds: Sc in each sc around.

18th rnd: [Dec, sc in next sc] 7 times, sc in next sc. 15 sc.

19th rnd: [Dec, sc in next sc] 5 times. 10 sc.

20th rnd: [Dec] 5 times. 5 sc.

Fasten off, using long tail to close hole.

Ear Pouf

1st rnd: Starting at the tip of the ear at Rnd 18, sl st D into stitches around the ear tip.

2nd rnd: Slip st in each slip st around. Fill in bare spots with D as needed.

Fasten off.

FINISHING

Sew head, tail, and sweater collar to body as in photo, using long yarn tails. Make certain parts are securely attached. Sew ears to head leaving approximately 4"/10cm diameter circle free between ears at top of head. Locate eye placement. Using black embroidery thread, sew 3 lines for eyelashes as shown. Attach buttons securely, overlapping the eyelashes a little OR embroider eyes if toy is to be used for children under 2 years of age.

Head Pouf

Add after ears have been attached and head has been sewn to neck.

1st rnd: Beginning at the crown of the head where the ears are attached, with larger hook and B, loosely work 25 slip sts into the sts of the Head in a circle about 4"/10cm diameter. This circle should be placed directly on top of the head, evenly spaced in conjunction with the ears.

2nd rnd: With D and larger hook, sc in each st around.

3rd rnd: Inc, [sc in next sc, inc] 12 times. 38 sc.

4th rnd: Sc in next 2 sc, [dec, sc in next 2 sc] 9 times. 29 sc.

5th rnd: [Dec, sc in next 3 sc] 5 times, dec, sc in last 2 sc. 23 sc.

6th rnd: Sc in next sc, [dec] 11 times. 12 sc.

7th rnd: [Dec] 6 times. 6 sc.

8th rnd: [Dec] 3 times. 3 sc.

Fasten off. Attach ribbon by weaving the tip between a few D sts, pulling through with even lengths and tying into a bow. Tighten and trim ends. •

PETAL BASKET

Easy

MEASUREMENTS

Approx 10"/25.5cm diameter × 6"/15cm high

MATERIALS

Yarn 

Bernat® *Baby Blanket™*, 10½oz/300g balls, each approx 220yd/201m (polyester)

- 2 balls in #04801 Misty Jungle Green (A)
- 1 ball in #04008 Vanilla (B)

Hook

- Size M/N-13 (9mm) crochet hook, *or size needed to obtain gauge*

Notion

- Stitch marker

GAUGE

7½ sc and 7 rows = 4"/10cm using size M/N-13 (9mm) hook with 2 strands held together.

TAKE TIME TO CHECK GAUGE.

BASKET

With 2 strands of A held tog, ch 2.

1st rnd: 8 sc in 2nd ch from hook. Join with sl st to first sc.

2nd rnd: Ch 1. 2 sc in each sc around. Join with sl st to first sc. 16 sc.

3rd rnd: Ch 1. *2 sc in next sc. 1 sc in next sc. Rep from * around. Join with sl st to rst sc. 24 sc.

4th rnd: Ch 1. *2 sc in next sc. 1 sc in each of next 2 sc. Rep from * around. Join with sl st to first sc. 32 sc.

5th rnd: Ch 1. *2 sc in next sc. 1 sc in each of next 3 sc. Rep from * around. Join with sl st to first sc. 40 sc.

6th rnd: Ch 1. *1 sc in each of next 2 sc. 2 sc in next sc. 1 sc in each of next 2 sc. Rep from * around. Join with sl st to rst sc. 48 sc.

7th rnd: Ch 1. *2 sc in next sc. 1 sc in each of next 5 sc. Rep from * around. Join with sl st to first sc. 56 sc.

8th rnd: Ch 1. *1 sc in each of next 3 sc. 2 sc in next sc. 1 sc in each of next 3 sc. Rep from * around. Join with sl st to rst sc. 64 sc.

9th rnd: Ch 1. *2 sc in next sc. 1 sc in each of next 7 sc. Rep from * around. Join with sl st to first sc. 72 sc.

10th rnd: Ch 1. *Working in back loops only,* 1 sc in each sc around. Join with sl st to first sc. Place marker at end of rnd.

11th rnd: Ch 1. *Working in both loops,* 1 sc in each sc around. Join with sl st to rst sc.

Rep last rnd until work from marked rnd measures 6"/15cm.

Next rnd: Ch 1. *Sc2tog. 1 sc in each of next 10 sc. Rep from * around. Join 2 strands of B with sl st to rst sc. 66 sc. Break A.

Next rnd: With B, ch 1. 1 sc in each sc around. Join with sl st to rst sc.

Next rnd: Ch 1. *Working in front loops only,* 1 sc in each

sc around. Join with sl st to rst sc. Turn.

Next rnd: (WS). Ch 1. 1 sc in each sc around. Join with sl st to rst sc. Turn.

FINISHING

First Petal

1st row: (RS). Ch 1. 2 sc in same st as last sl st. 1 sc in each of next 9 sc. 2 sc in next sc. 13 sc. Turn. Leave rem sts unworked.

2nd and 3rd rows: Ch 1. 1 sc in each sc to end of row. Turn.

4th row: Ch 1. Sc2tog. 1 sc in each of next 9 sc. Sc2tog. 11 sc.

5th row: Ch 1. Sc2tog. 1 sc in each of next 7 sc. Sc2tog. 9 sc.

6th row: Ch 1. (Sc2tog) twice. 1 sc in next sc. (Sc2tog) twice. 5 sc.

Fasten off.

Second through Sixth Petals

With RS facing, join 2 strands of B with sl st to rst unworked st of last rnd of Basket. Work 1st to 6th rows as given for First Petal. •

SHEEP MOBILE

Easy

MEASUREMENTS

Each sheep measures approx 4½"/11.5cm long.

MATERIALS

Yarn 

Bernat® *Baby Velvet™*, 10½oz/300g balls, each approx 492yd/450m (polyester)

- 1 ball in #86018 Cuddly Cloud (A)
- 1 ball in #86020 Ever After Pink (B)

Note: 1 ball of A and B will make approx 20 Sheep.

Hook

- Size G/6 (4mm) crochet hook, *or size needed to obtain gauge*

Notions

- Stuffing
- 2¼"/0.5cm diameter dowels cut to 12"/30.5 cm
- Monofilament fishing line

GAUGE

14 sc and 15 rows = 4" [10 cm].

TAKE TIME TO CHECK GAUGE.

STITCH GLOSSARY

Beg Bobble = Ch 3. (Yoh and draw up a loop. Yoh and draw through 2 loops on hook) twice. Yoh and draw through all loops on hook.

Bobble = (Yoh and draw up a loop. Yoh and draw through 2 loops on hook) 3 times in indicated sp. Yoh and draw through all loops on hook.

NOTE

Join each rnd with sl st to first st.

SHEEP (MAKE 5)

With B, ch 2.

1st rnd: 6 sc in 2nd ch from hook. Join.

2nd rnd: Ch 1. 1 sc in each sc around. Join.

3rd rnd: Ch 1. 2 sc in each sc around. Join.12 sc.

4th rnd: Ch 1. 1 sc in first sc. Ch 4. 1 sc in 2nd ch from hook. 1 sc in each of next 2 ch. 1 sc in each of next 5 sc. Ch 4. 1 sc in 2nd ch from hook. 1 sc in each of next 2 ch. 1 sc in each of next 6 sc. Join A with sl st to back loop only of first st. Break B.

5th rnd: With A, ch 1. *Working in back loops only,* 2 sc in first sc. 1 sc in next sc. *2 sc in next sc. 1 sc in next sc. Rep from * around. Join. 18 sc.

6th rnd: *Working in both loops,* beg Bobble in first sc. 1 sc in each of next 2 dc. *Bobble in next sc. 1 sc in each of next 2 sc. Rep from * around. Join.

7th rnd: Ch 1. 2 sc in first st. 1 sc in each of next 2 sts. *2 sc in next st. 1 sc in each of next 2 sts. Rep from * around. Join. 24 sc.

8th rnd: Ch 1. 1 sc in each of first 3 sc. Bobble in next sc. *1 sc in each of next 3 sc. Bobble in next sc. Rep from * around. Join.

9th rnd: Ch 1. 2 sc in first st. 1 sc in each of next 3 sts. *2 sc in next st. 1 sc in each of next 3 sts. Rep from * around. Join. 30 sc.

10th rnd: Ch 1. 1 sc in each of first 2 sc. *Bobble in next sc. 1 sc in each of next 4 sc. Rep from * to last 2 sc. 1 sc in each of last 2 sc. Join.

11th rnd: Ch 1. *Sc2tog. 1 sc in each of next 3 sts. Rep from * around. Join. 24 sc.

12th rnd: Beg Bobble in first sc. 1 sc in each of next 3 sc. *Bobble in next sc. 1 sc in each of next 3 sc. Rep from * around. Join.

13th rnd: Ch 1. *Sc2tog. 1 sc in each of next 2 sts. Rep from * around. 18 sc. Join.

14th rnd: Ch 1. 1 sc in each of first 2 sc. Bobble in next sc. *1 sc in each of next 2 sc. Bobble in next sc. Rep from * around. Join.

15th rnd: Ch 1. *Sc2tog. 1 sc in next st. Rep from * around. 12 sc. Join. Stuff Sheep.

16th rnd: Ch 1. *Sc2tog. Rep from * around. 6 sc. Fasten off. Thread end through rem sts and cinch tightly.

Legs (Make 4 per Sheep)

With B, ch 5.

1st row: Sl st in 2nd ch from hook. Sl st in each of next 3 ch.

Fasten off.

HEARTS (MAKE 10)

With B, ch 2.

1st rnd: 5 sc in 2nd ch from hook. Join.

2nd rnd: Ch 1. 2 sc in first sc. (1 hdc. 1 dc. 1 tr. 1 dc. 1 hdc) in next sc. Sl st in next sc. (1 hdc. 1 dc. 1 tr. 1 dc. 1 hdc) in next sc. 2 sc in next sc. Ch 2. Sl st in 2nd ch from hook. Join.

Fasten off.

FINISHING

Sew 4 Legs to each Sheep as seen in picture. Cut 5 lengths of monofilament fish line approx 15"/38cm long. Thread 2 Hearts and one Sheep on each thread and tie to dowels as seen in picture. •

VELVET BUNNY

Intermediate

MEASUREMENTS

Approx 15"/38cm tall

MATERIALS

Yarn (4)

Bernat® *Baby Velvet*™, 10½oz/300g balls, each approx 492yd/450m (polyester)

- 1 ball in #86018 Cuddly Cloud (A)
- 1 ball in #86020 Ever After Pink (B)

Hook

- Size G/6 (4mm) crochet hook, *or size needed to obtain gauge*

Notions

- Polyester fiberfill.
- Small amount of black embroidery floss for eyes.

GAUGE

16 sc and 17 rows = 4"/10cm using size G/6 (4mm) hook.

TAKE TIME TO CHECK GAUGE.

NOTE

- Join all rnds with sl st to first st.

FIRST LEG

Note: Leg is worked beg at foot.

With B, ch 7.

1st rnd: 1 sc in 2nd ch from hook. 1 sc in each of next 4 ch. 3 sc in last ch. *Do not* turn. *Working in rem loops of foundation ch,* 1 sc in each of next 4 ch. 2 sc in last ch. Join. 14 sc.

2nd rnd: Ch 1. 2 sc in first sc. 1 sc in each of next 4 sc. 2 sc in each of next 3 sc. 1 sc in each of next 4 sc. 2 sc in each of next 2 sc. Join. 20 sc.

3rd rnd: Ch 1. 2 sc in first sc. 1 sc in each of next 6 sc. 2 sc in each of next 4 sc. 1 sc in each of next 6 sc. 2 sc in each of next 2 sc. Join. 26 sc.

4th rnd: Ch 1. 1 sc in each sc around. Break B. Join A.

5th rnd: With A, ch 1. *Working in back loops only,* 1 sc in each sc around. Join.

6th to 8th rnds: Ch 1. *Working in both loops,* 1 sc in each sc around. Join.

9th rnd: Ch 1. 1 sc in each of next 6 sc. (Sc2tog) 6 times. 1 sc in each of next 8 sc. Join. 20 sts.

10th rnd: Ch 1. 1 sc in each of next 7 sc. (Sc2tog) twice. 1 sc in each of next 9 sc. Join. 18 sts.

11th rnd: Ch 1. 1 sc in each st around. Join. 18 sc.

12th rnd: Ch 1. 1 sc in each sc around. Join.

Rep last rnd until Leg measures approx 5"/12.5cm from 5th rnd. Fasten off.

SECOND LEG

Work as given for First Leg. *Do not* fasten off.

Stuff Legs. Cont as follows for Body:

BODY

Join Legs

1st rnd: With A, ch 1. 1 sc in each of next 7 sc. 1 sc in first sc of First leg. 1 sc in each sc of First leg around.
1 sc in each of rem 12 sc of Second Leg.
Join. 36 sc.

2nd rnd: Ch 1. 1 sc in each of next 6 sc. 2 sc in each of next 2 sc. 1 sc in each of next 16 sc. 2 sc in each of next 2 sc. 1 sc in each sc to end of rnd. Join. 40 sc.

3rd rnd: Ch 1. 1 sc in each sc around. Join.

4th rnd: Ch 1. 1 sc in each of next 27 sc. 2 sc in each of next 2 sc. 1 sc in each sc to end of rnd. Join. 42 sc.

5th to 16th rnds: As 3rd rnd.

17th rnd: Ch 1. 1 sc in each of next 21 sc. (1 sc in next sc.
Sc2tog) 7 times. Join. 35 sts.

18th rnd: As 3rd rnd.

19th rnd: Ch 1. (Sc2tog. 1 sc in each of next 5 sc) 3 times.
1 sc in each sc to end of rnd.
Join. 32 sts.

20th rnd: As 3rd rnd.

21st rnd: Ch 1. *Sc2tog. 1 sc in each of next 6 sts. Rep from * around. Join. 28 sts.

22nd rnd: As 3rd rnd.

23rd rnd: Ch 1. *Sc2tog. 1 sc in next 2 sc. Rep from * around. Join. 21 sts.

24th rnd: As 3rd rnd.

25th rnd: Ch 1. (Sc2tog. 1 sc in each of next 5 sc) 3 times. Join. 18 sts.

26th rnd: As 3rd rnd. Fasten off.

Stuff Body.

ARMS (MAKE 2)

With A, ch 2.

1st rnd: 8 sc in 2nd ch from hook. Join. 8 sc.

2nd rnd: Ch 1. 2 sc in each sc in each sc around. Join. 16 sc.

3rd rnd: Ch 1. 2 sc in first sc. 1 sc in each of next 7 sc.

VELVET BUNNY

2 sc in next sc. 1 sc in each sc to end of rnd. Join. 18 sc.

4th to 8th rnds: Ch 1. 1 sc in each sc around. Join.

9th rnd: Ch 1. (Sc2tog. 1 sc in each of next 7 sc) twice. Join. 16 sts.

10th to 12th rnds: Ch 1. 1 sc in each st around. Join.

13th rnd: Ch 1. *Sc2tog. 1 sc in each of next 2 sc. Rep from * around. Join. 12 sts.

14th rnd: Ch 1. 1 sc in each st around. Join.

Rep last rnd 10 times more. Fasten off.

Stuff Arms.

HEAD

With A, ch 2.

1st rnd: 8 sc in 2nd ch from hook. Join. 8 sc.

2nd rnd: Ch 1. 2 sc in each sc around. Join. 16 sc.

3rd rnd: Ch 1. *2 sc in next sc. 1 sc in next sc. Rep from * around. Join. 24 sc.

4th rnd: Ch 1. *2 sc in next sc. 1 sc in each of next 2 sc. Rep from * around. Join. 32 sc.

5th rnd: Ch 1. 1 sc in each sc around. Join.

6th rnd: Ch 1. *2 sc in next sc. 1 sc in each of next 3 sc. Rep from * around. Join. 40 sc.

7th rnd: As 5th rnd.

Rep last rnd 7 times more.

Next rnd: Ch 1. *Sc2tog. 1 sc in each of next 3 sc. Rep from * around. Join. 32 sts.

Next rnd: Ch 1. *Sc2tog. 1 sc in each of next 2 sc. Rep from * around. Join. 24 sts.

Next rnd: Ch 1. *Sc2tog. 1 sc in next sc. Rep from * around. Join. 16 sts. Fasten off. Stuff Head.

OUTER EAR (MAKE 2)

With A, ch 5.

1st row: 1 sc in 2nd ch from hook. 1 sc in each ch to end of ch. Turn. 4 sc.

2nd row: Ch 1. 2 sc in first sc. 1 sc in each of next 4 sc. 2 sc in last sc. Turn. 6 sc.

3rd and 4th rows: Ch 1. 1 sc in each sc to end of row. Turn.

5th row: Ch 1. 2 sc in first sc. 1 sc in each of next 6 sc. 2 sc in last sc. Turn. 8 sc.

6th and 7th rows: As 3rd and 4th rows.

8th row: Ch 1. 2 sc in first sc. 1 sc in each of next 8 sc. 2 sc in last sc. Turn. 10 sc.

9th to 20th rows: Ch 1. 1 sc in each sc to end of row. Turn.

21st row: Ch 1. Sc2tog. 1 sc in each of next 6 sc. Sc2tog. Turn. 8 sts.

23rd row: Ch 1. Sc2tog. 1 sc in each of next 4 sc. Sc2tog. Turn. 6 sts.

24th row: Ch 1. Sc2tog. 1 sc in each of next 2 sc. Sc2tog. Turn. 4 sts.

25th row: Ch 1. (Sc2tog) twice. Fasten off.

Edging

Join A with sl st to bottom right corner of Ear. Ch 1. Work sc evenly up right side of Ear, having 3 sc in tip of Ear, then down left side. Fasten off.

INNER EAR (MAKE 2)

With B, work as given for Outer Ear.

Join Ears

With WS of Inner and Outer Ear tog, join A with sl st to bottom right corner of Ear. *Working through both thicknesses,* work 1 sc in each sc to join Outer and Inner Ear, having 3 sc in center sc at tip of Ear. Fasten off.

FINISHING

Sew Ears to top of Head as shown in picture. With black embroidery floss, embroider eyes using satin stitch. With B, embroider nose and mouth using straight stitch. Attach Head and Arms to Body.•

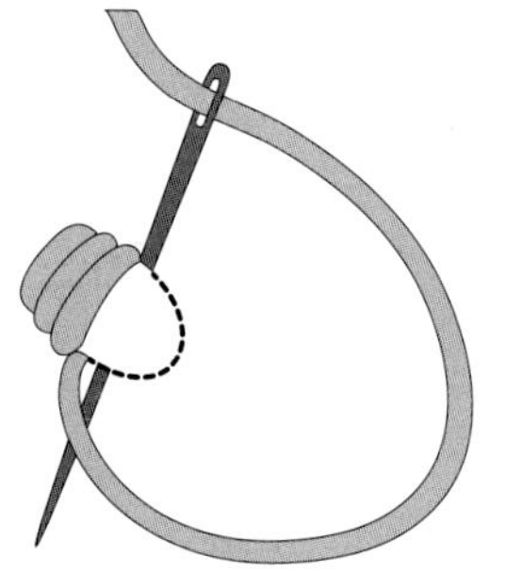

SATIN STITCH

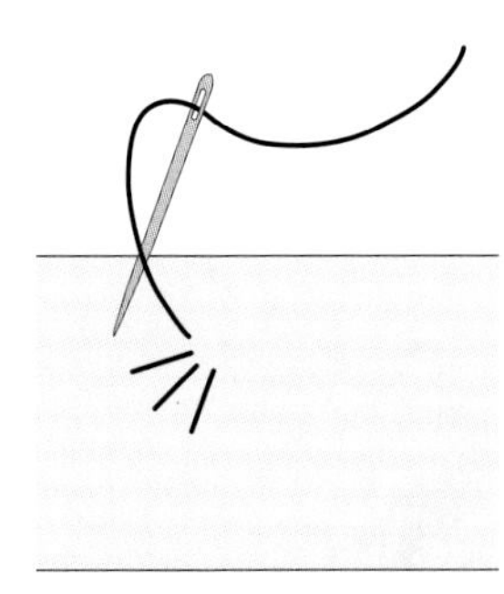

STRAIGHT STITCH